KHONT-HON-NOFER
The Lands of Ethiopia

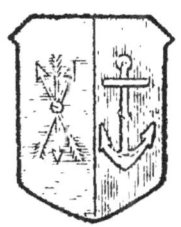

The arrows Faith, Hope, and Love, winged by the Holy Ghost, will reach the heart of the Dark Continent, and the Cross surmounting the Crescent must form our anchor of hope for Africa.

BY
H. K. W. KUMM, Ph.D.

Author of " Tribes of the Nile Valley '
" The Political Economy of Nubia"
" The Sudan"
" From Hausaland to Egypt"

Copyright © 2018 Read Books Ltd.
This book is copyright and may not be
reproduced or copied in any way without
the express permission of the publisher in writing

British Library Cataloguing-in-Publication Data
A catalogue record for this book is available from
the British Library

PREFACE

AT the outset of this book describing the findings of the writer in Central Africa during last year's journey, as far as they relate to the ethical and religious questions of these lands, he desires to emphasise his deep feeling of gratitude, and to express his indebtedness to the many in the British Isles and across the sea who have followed him with their prayers and made the seeming impossibilities possible; among them the missionaries of the Church Missionary Society in Northern Nigeria and his fellow labourers, of the Sudan United Mission in Africa and America, as well as in England and on the Continent. As the writer passed grave after grave of explorers, scientists, Government officials and traders; as he was warned by Government men repeatedly not to continue or he would probably not return; as he remembers the climatic dangers, the dangers from wild beasts and the yet more dangerous representatives of the human race;

PREFACE

> "Gefaerlich ist's den Leu zu wecken,
> Und toetlich ist des Tiger's Zahn
> Doch all das Schreckliste der Schrecken
> Das ist der Mensch in seinem Wahn;"

as he looks back to the days and weeks of torrential rains, of miasma-breeding swamps, impassable rivers and impossible tribes, he realises with a deep feeling of humility the goodness of God and the faithfulness of his friends.

H.K.W.K.

16 New Bridge Street,
   London, E.C.

CONTENTS

	PAGE
PREFACE	vii

CHAPTER I.
    The Baby Nations of the World - - - 1

CHAPTER II.
    Preparations for a Trans-African Journey - - 17

CHAPTER III.
    A Lesson in Geography, and a Visit to the Sudan United Mission Stations - - - - 31

CHAPTER IV.
    A Day's Work - - - - - - 55

CHAPTER V.
    From Northern Nigeria to the Nile.—From the Benué to Bor - - - - - - 71

CHAPTER VI.
    Hunting in Africa: Slaves and Animals (Freed Slaves' Home) - - - - - - 89

CHAPTER VII.
    Mohammedanism, with a Short History of Sinussiism - - - - - - - 111

CONTENTS

CHAPTER VIII.
 Heathenism in the Sudan - - - - - 133

CHAPTER IX.
 History of Missions in the Sudan - - - 157

CHAPTER X.
 The Success or Otherwise of Missions in Central Africa - - - - - - - - - 179

CHAPTER XI.
 Missionary Politics: True Christian Imperialism   199

CHAPTER XII.
 Strategic Points of the Sudan - - - - 215

CHAPTER XIII.
 Conclusion.—At Gordon's Statue.—The Sphinx.   237

APPENDICES

(A)   Missionaries in the Sudan - - - - 245
(B)   Bibliography of the Sudan - - - - 253
(C)   Map - - - - - - - - - 284
(D)   Index - - - - - - - - 283

LIST OF ILLUSTRATIONS

1. The Sphinx and the Pyramids in the Chamsin
FRONTISPIECE

                                        PAGE

2. Dr. Gustav Nachtigal, who carried the first Bibles into the Central Soudan - - - - 38

3. Lieutenant Boyd Alexander, killed at Nyeri - 39

4. Dr. Kumm and a French Trader in a Forest Camp in the unexplored - - - - 63

5. Sultan Muhamed, of Wadda, a notorious slave trader - - - - - - - - 84

6. The Lucy Memorial Freed Slaves' Home at Rumàsha, Northern Nigeria - - - 103

7. Girls' Class at the Lucy Memorial Home - - 108

8. Sultan Sinussi of Ndele at the French Government Post - - - - - - - - 130

9. The Chief of Wukari, a friend of the Missionaries 136

10. A Juju Hut in a Sara-Kabba Village - - - 147

11. Slaves in the Shari Region liberated by Captain Faure, after a severe fight with their captors 213

12. Sphinx - - - - - - - - 243

13. Map of Dr. Kumm's Journey - - - - 284

To
the Nations
of the Future
the Races yet to be.

The Baby Nations of the World

"Where there is no vision,
the people perish."
Prov. xxix. 18.

CHAPTER I

INTRODUCTION

*What is it that walks
"In the morn on four,
At noon on two,
At night on three?"*

THE riddle of the Sphinx, which was propounded, so mythology tells us, at the dawn of the ages, by the man-beast to the children of men!

What is it?

It is man!

Physical man; leaving out of count for a moment his soul life.

Crawling in its childhood days close to the ground with its face to the dust, the weakest, most ignorant and all but instinctless of animals.

Look at it again in thirty years at the noonday of life, erect, with its face to the sun, ruling creation, in its eyes the fire-light of the Spirit of God.

Man.

Look at it again! But a few years have gone, and the strong, straight backbone is bent, the steel-hard blood-swelled muscles have become flabby; with a crutch or a crooked stick slowly it toils along, sinking gradually back to the earth whence it came!

Developed Parallelism of Laplace.

Like the life of a man, the life of a nation is a progress from childhood to old age; and similar marks characterise both. The innocence, the credulity, the trustfulness, the enterprise and boldness that we find in childhood we find among the baby nations of the world; as we find deliberateness in action, slowness in movement, lack of trust in self amongst the senile peoples of the globe, such as the Egyptians, the Armenians, the Tibetans, the Koreans. The Arian race, especially the youngest branch of it—the Anglo-Saxon—is to-day in the full strength of its manhood, while in Africa and in the South Sea Islands we have the infants of our human family. The irresponsibility, credulity, and simplicity of most of the tribes in Central Africa are the unmistakable signs of youthfulness.

It is in the childhood of a people that religious impressions are most easily received, and influence its development. Not only in the human life is it the child that most readily and naturally turns to and follows the Saviour. And the words of the Master, "Suffer little children to come unto Me, and forbid them not, for of such is the kingdom of Heaven," hold good for the young races of the world.

"The time for Africa is not yet."

The thought which one has heard expressed by a leading man in foreign missionary enterprise, that "*the time for Africa is not yet*," appears incorrect. "Give me the education of the child up to the

BABY NATIONS OF THE WORLD

age of seven," said Cardinal Manning, "and he will be a Roman Catholic for life." It is in the days of childhood that character is formed.

"Acts create a habit, habits a character, character a destiny." To train an old oak and bend its trunk is a practical impossibility, but the oak-sapling will obey the trainer's hand and bow to his will. To graft valuable fruit cuttings into an old tree is something a wise gardener does not go in for. For satisfactory and profitable grafting strong young trees are needed. It is perfectly right that the young tree swerves in the wind while the trunk of a five-hundred-year-old giant of the forest is solid and immovable. If you graft on to a young tree the wind may break the tree and make your labour in vain; if you graft on to an old tree the wind will not hurt your tree, but your labour will not be rewarded with the very permanent and satisfactory results you are justified in looking for in the former case. *Parables.*

An old man may be converted to God, but his habits and his character, while they may be altered, can only be altered by a manifest miracle, which is not needed to the same extent in the child. Nine-tenths of our Christians to-day can trace their Christianity back to their childhood, and the one-tenth which is the exception simply proves the rule, that we are to aim at the young if we desire to add steadily to our churches.

How is it, then, that the young nations of the world are out of fashion? How is it that the proportion of men and money designated for the baby races of the world is insignificant as *Unfashionable Children.*

compared with the number of workers and funds used amongst the peoples that can look back upon three or four millenniums?

We are unconsciously imitating the fashions of the West-end of London. The babies of the house, and the growing children of "awkward age," live in a shut-off part of the building; they are not allowed in the drawing-room. The naked negroes of Central Africa, despised and neglected, will grow up to manhood some day, and it will then appear whether it was worth while that, in their childhood days, they were won for the Christian faith.

Thank God for the revivals in Korea and in India; but these nations have passed through their zenith, they have culminated. Youthful garments will not give an old man back his nervous energy and his physical vigour; and the European civilisation, now thrown as a cloak over the decadent and declining tribes of mankind in the East, cannot hide the corroding effects of immorality indulged in for centuries. The unclad morally clean savages of the mountains and plains, of the deserts and swamps of Central Africa, have not yet been looked upon as a people with a future, as the rising ones.

From my early days I preferred the straightforward fighter to the sly assassin. If the negro desires to kill his man, he does so in a remarkably blunt way. There is no finesse in the blackamoor, with a stone or an axe braining his enemy. But the Mongol and the Indian is of a different make-up, at least so one gathers from the story of the Boxer riots and of the Indian mutiny; the flaying alive, the poisonings, the tortures. This straightforwardness and simplicity in warfare is again a sign of youth. The negro is the "hobble-dehoy" of the human family. The stripling who does not know how to behave himself, who has plenty of brawn and comparatively little brain, but who, with his years, will outgrow his clumsiness. And the six-foot three Dinka, and the six-foot four Shilluk, and the six-foot five Musgun will come to their inheritance some day, as well as the Zulu, the Barotsi, and the Baganda. *The Hobbledehoy of the Human Family.*

Arguing from the relative present and problematic future value of the races, the time for the evangelisation of the Central African is now, when, for the first time, he is coming into contact with the emissaries of European civilisation, Christian or otherwise. We shall see, as we progress, the special claims which Central Africa has upon our day and generation.

Given peace and protection, no other race multiplies like the black race. Their children will inherit a good part of the earth. Let us see to it that, through them, the human family advances towards the ideal. *Fecundity of the Negro.*

It seems to have escaped many students of foreign missions, that the history of our own race teaches us a lesson. There are no two opinions that the three Protestant Christian nations, Britain, Germany, and the United States control the world. We became, through the Bible and Christianity, what we are. At what period was Christianity introduced amongst our forefathers?

Was it after they had attained to a high state of civilisation? Was it after they had established a civilised commonwealth commanding the respect of the world? Was it after millenniums of intellectual development? Or was it in the days—the early baby days—of the infancy of our race?

Rome was a civilised empire with a past, an empire decadent, and, in spite of Christianity being grafted upon it, the decay was not stayed.

Imperial Rome broke up.

Our Forefathers. In West Central Europe there lived a race of healthy woodsmen without a history, without a past; woodsmen with a strong physique, a moral people amongst whom the woman was the priestess of the family, and if a youth forgot himself so far as to commit adultery, the punishment was that he was thrown into a ditch, a hurdle placed over his head, and he was choked in the stagnant mud.

This was the material out of which Christianity formed the world Empires of the Teuton and Anglo-Saxon races.

Is there no lesson in this? Of course, missionary work amongst a heathen civilised people, is much more satisfactory and promising at the time. An Indian or a Chinese convert to Christianity is a full-grown man; a savage Central African convert to Christianity is a baby. But the baby has a future, while the old man has a past. The Gospel should be preached to the grown-up people, but the future is with the baby races of the world. These views have lately crystallised in me into convictions. They have not been adequately recognised in the past, yet should form one of the fundamental principles in the policy of our foreign missionary enterprise. To despise and disregard missionary work among the child nations because they are children, and because it will take generations before they grow up into spiritual manhood, is the parallel to the treatment vouchsafed to the children of the British Isles in legislation at the beginning of the nineteenth century.

The British Dominions, Canada, South Africa, Australia, New Zealand, the children of the Empire, are not despised and neglected. The younger Colonies, if promising, receive the greatest attention. In communal life the care taken of the young is now recognised as one of the most important privileges and duties of a community. In Church life at home the Sunday School is looked upon as the nursery of the Church.

Children in National, Communal, and Church Life.

One of the teachers in my school days was wont to say to his class that he looked upon every boy with respect, and that he felt his responsibility to be great, as he might have, unknown to him, the shaping of the destiny of a future Napoleon or Martin Luther in his control.

The present, in national, Church, and individual life, is controlled by the manhood of our race, but the future lies embedded in the young.

It has frequently been suggested that the coloured people are not capable of attaining to a civilisation such as the Indo-Germanic races have evolved. Careful investigation shows us that this is not so. The Egyptian is an old, civilised, white, Semitic nation, but the youthful, ignorant Sudanese is his superior as a fighter. Rudyard Kipling, in his quaint but telling way, when speaking of the Sudanese, says:—

> "The Fuzzy-wuzzy,
> At his home in the Sudan,
> Is a poor benighted heathen
> But a first-class fighting man."

And, comparing him with other warriors which have been encountered by British troops, such as the Boers, the Pathans in the north of India, and the Burmese, the woolly-headed son of the Sudan excels in the respect he secured from the British Tommy Atkins.

As to educational qualifications, surely men like Booker Washington, like Bishop Crowther, and King Khama of Bechuanaland, must be reckoned as intelligent men who are the forerunners of a coming race, such as Ulfilas was for the Goths, Winifred Boniface for the Germans, Augustine, Patrick, and Columba for the British Isles. What the Franks and Irish were among the Arian people, the Baganda, the Hausas, and the Yorubas are in Africa, the vanguard of the advancing negro nations.

Vanguard. The misunderstanding of the black people which has come, and is coming to us, from the United States will be no blessing to the British Empire. The American is the youngest son of the Anglo-Saxon family, and a very healthy youth he is, a mixture of the most enterprising manhood of Europe, with a certain seasoning of the undesirable elements of the old world. Having in an ecstatic fit of enthusiasm for liberty, abolished slavery and turned out the slaves into the highways and byeways, America prepared for herself a problem, the solution of which will not be within this or the next generation. What America did, while trying to do her best for the slaves, was a cruel injustice to a child-race that had not been trained up to self-restraint and independence. How very much more satisfactory the results would have been, and all the race hatred, the lynching, and sacrificing of coloured criminals avoided, had the trade and traffic in slaves been abolished, and domestic slavery gradually come to an end, through the compulsory education of the free children of domestic slaves, or the establishment of one or two free negro states under the control of wise, white administrators.

The negro population cannot now be eliminated from the United States, but is becoming part and parcel of that new *Anglo-Saxon-Celtic-Indian-Hamitic-Semitic* world power. The negroes of the States, with a few exceptions, being descendants of slaves, are originally not negroes of the highest type. The strong, liberty-loving free tribes in the Sudan and in parts of South Africa could not, and cannot be enslaved. They may be captured, but, when captured, they will die. As a rule neither the strongest, nor the most intellectual, become slaves. **The Freeborn.**

If, therefore, the coloured people in the United States have been able to produce a Booker Washington, a William H. Lewis, and others, what may we not be justified in expecting when the children of the Continent of Sunshine —for such, rather, than the Dark Continent would I name the Continent of Africa—enter seriously into the race for the goal of the highest civilisation ?

We have seen that they are first-class fighting men. They certainly produce orators. They are

Race Assets natural musicians. It can hardly be said that the Africans have not produced leaders of men, though the percentage of such leaders up to the present may be small. So far from ceding that the Bantus and the Hamitic people lack the qualifications for the highest development, the writer ventures to suggest that all the rudimentary elements that made the Anglo-Saxon race what it is to-day are found in the negro, and qualities even beyond those of our forefathers.

The woman amongst the negroes is free. The wife of the Arab, the Indian and the Mongol, in the majority of cases, is either maintained soulless or a slave. There are, of course, exceptions to the rule. There are black tribes where the women are slaves, and there are Eastern people amongst whom the women are on the same level as the man. But these are few and far between.

Six years ago, when I travelled in Northern Nigeria, I was introduced by the chief of the Jukun village Dempar, to the village god whose name was Dodo. Whenever Dodo was mentioned amongst my followers, a smile flitted over their faces. There seemed to be some curious connection between the women and Dodo.

And when the chief of Dempar called on me, and I requested information on the famous spirit, the chief looked shy and then slightly amused. It took some time before he could be persuaded to let out the Dodo secret, but after a while he explained that Dodo was a god clothed in cock's feathers, and that none of the women were allowed to see Dodo. Dodo usually came once a month, and announced his presence by drumming and crowing. Immediately all the women would hide, as to see Dodo or be seen by him meant death to them. At a certain age all the boys of the tribe would be initiated by a special Dodo ceremony into the secrets of this society. Dodo was a very powerful spirit. I suggested to his dusky majesty that Dodo was a fraud, and nothing but a man dressed up. And after some hesitancy my coloured friend agreed with me.

<small>Dodo.</small>

Then ensued the following conversation.

H. M. "But you know, white man, we need Dodo."

The Writer. "Why"?

H. M. "It is difficult enough to make our women obey now. What would we do if we had not Dodo to frighten them with? They would just rule us."

Here was certainly a case in which "mere man" felt it necessary to protect himself by a specially designated god against his better half.

I fully realise that amongst the Northern tribes of India there are some that must be reckoned as child nations, and that in the interior of China there are certain families of the Mongol race that can hardly be said to have culminated. But taken as a whole, a student of history must agree that the Mongols culminated under Djengis-khan in the thirteenth century, when they attempted the conquest of Europe; and while victorious in the battle of Lignitz lost so many that they were compelled to return to the steppes of Central Asia.

China.

India, one of the cradles of the human races, attained its utmost splendour under the great Mohgul. As nations, units in the race for world power, China and India have had their day.

India.

Japan presents a more difficult problem, but the untrustworthiness and physical decadence of the Japanese, a result of a low type of morality, look very much as if the suddenly displayed marvellous energy is only an abnormal flare-up of the dying fire of national life.

Japan.

I am perfectly aware that these views are opposed to the commonly accepted theories and ideas held by political and missionary leaders, but I venture to advance them, as they contain arguments that are well worth considering.

"*Audite alteram partem.*"

God has entrusted the Britons with more of the youthful peoples of this earth than any other white race. We are trustees, appointed by God, to shield the little ones, to teach them and to mother them until they have grown up into independence.

The two or three hundred different heathen clans amongst whom we are to-day administering justice in Central Africa, are in our hands as little children whose fate and future we may make or mar. If we prove ourselves unworthy trustees we shall be charged with the issues of our stewardship. Justice, truthfulness, honesty and liberty are valued more highly in Britain than in any other state on earth; and it is on this account that God has seen fit to give us charge of the development of many of the native races of Central Africa, Asia, America, and Australasia.

> "He Who made us mighty,
> Make us mightier yet!"

in righteousness and godlikeness.

Preparations for a Trans-African Journey

Four Rules of Life of General Gordon:

1. Shelve the "I" entirely.
2. Renounce all claims to recognition.
3. Never make praise or blame the cause of your action.
4. In all things build on GOD.

CHAPTER II

IT may appear presumptuous and self-assertive to begin the second chapter with a short autobiography, yet people have asked so often about preparations and qualifications for Mission work in Central Africa, and travelling and exploring, that I feel justified, with these remarks, and my humble apology, to submit the following :—

In the days when, as a schoolboy, I grew up in the Hartz mountains of Hanover, I had three ambitions, namely, that I might learn to ride well on horseback, swim well, and shoot well. If a boy's ambitions are strong enough they will more or less influence his life as a man. Living in a little town surrounded by great pine forests, there was every opportunity for the youngster to indulge in ambitions that had to do with his physical life.

A Boy's Ambition.

The ozone of the woods, the deer and wild boar of the mountains, and morally clean companions, as well as the simple home-life, could not but influence my bodily development. I learned to shoot when I was about fourteen years of age, but for riding and swimming, opportunities were few. These came later.

I was almost twenty years of age before I left home and the regular routine of school life. History and mathematics were my favourite subjects; modern languages had no terrors for me, but Latin was a trial to the flesh, and the ten years I spent over it failed to make me perfect. But natural history I delighted in, and I preserve to this day my butterfly collections, my Herbarium, my collection of beetles and birds' eggs, minerals and laboratory tools. There was no hawk's nest too high and no cave too deep if new specimens might be secured. To go out after school hours in the afternoon, tramp five or six miles to some far-off mountain meadow, and there stalk the stags and watch them feeding; to start out on half-holidays in the winter when the snow was three feet deep to some feeding place in the forest where the wild boars used to congregrate, or to build up a camp fire in some charcoal-burner's hut, and there indulge in roasting potatoes or in a forbidden pipe of tobacco, were the land-marks of a life privileged as few are, to grow up and develop in such surroundings.

It was the forest born physique that malaria and dysentery, appendicitis and the low fever of Central Africa have not been able to break up.

Mental Preparation. As to the mental preparation for exploring Africa, I have mentioned already my love of natural history, and the comparative ease with which I acquired modern languages. To English, German and French, Arabic and Hausa, the two leading languages of Africa, were added.

A TRANS-AFRICAN JOURNEY

A mathematical mind made the study of astronomy comparatively easy, and Time and Place observations gave me no trouble. My main subject in the Examination for the degree of Doctor of Philosophy being geography, geology, meteorology and political economy were necessary, besides astronomy, Semitic languages and philosophy. A little medical knowledge, just enough to be able to use the main remedies for the African diseases, was found most useful.

As to ethical preparations, these were acquired in a slow and continuous process. Loneliness has no terrors for me. The trees of the woods were the companions of my childhood, and a period away from the society of my fellow-men I welcome rather than otherwise. *Ethical Preparations.*

Descending from a military family, obedience was inborn. Having early learned to accommodate myself to the control of others, be it parent or teacher, I had thus secured the first qualification for leadership, for he who has not learned to obey will never lead. Travellers and explorers have frequently complained about the difficulties they had with their carriers and followers. To me on my journeys, such were conspicuous by their absence. There was no playing about with my followers. Once a command was issued it was obeyed. Leaving out punctuality, which from the native of Central Africa I have never been able to secure, simple respect and obedience were never wanting from my people. *Leadership*

As to former journeyings and work in Africa, I was greatly favoured by being able to secure

Earlier Journeyings.

an incidental knowledge and insight into the political relationship of the various European Colonies, into the religions, both Moslem, and Pagan as well as Christian, and into the missionary operations. A concomitant geographical knowledge was the natural outcome of my journeyings.

Two years and a half I spent in Egypt in the study of Arabic, in work amongst Moslems, and in itineration in the delta and oases of the Fayoum, Charga, Dachla, and Beriis. Later, two visits to Nubia and a visit to Palestine widened my experience. Then came a journey to Tripoli with the study of the Hausa language, and certain investigations in the mountains which no Christian interested in missionary work had visited for over a thousand years. The ruins of marble palaces, colleges and churches are monuments of a golden age that has passed away under the stagnating influence of the Moslem rule in the Turkish provinces of Tripoli. It was my privilege to visit a number of Mohammedan Senussi sauvijas* in the neighbourhood of Gebel-Grurian in the interior of Tripoli. The natives were exceptionally fanatical, and once or twice I was threatened, and once actually shot at without having given any provocation whatsoever. Tunis and Algiers were also traversed on this fourth North African journey.

The fifth journey took me to the West Coast of Africa, and through the coast regions to Northern Nigeria. I had been asked by

* Pronounced *zaw-we-ya*.

Professor Dove, of Jena University, to write a couple of Essays on the hydrography of the regions of the Guinea Coast and the British Colony of Northern Nigeria. A certain amount of geographical research work, besides investigations into the advance of Mohammedanism among the pagan tribes of those regions and the building of the first Mission Station of the Sudan United Mission, as well as a visit through the Murchison Range and Bautchi Plateau, added considerably to my knowledge of Paganism and Mohammedanism in West Central Africa, as well as to my botanical and zoological knowledge of those lands.

The sixth and last and longest journey was a tour round the Continent. Coming down the West Coast, I landed at Cape Town, traversed Cape Colony, the Orange River Colony, Transvaal and Natal, visiting most of the important towns and villages, and addressing some dozens of audiences on the advance of Mohammendanism in Central Africa. Later, I continued my journey by way of Delagoa Bay, Beira, Mozambique, German East Africa, Zanzibar; then went up from Mombasa, through British East Africa by way of Nairobi to Lake Victoria and Uganda; returned thence to attend a Missionary Conference at Kijabe, the Central Station of the Africa Inland Mission, where some thirty-five missionaries of the Church Missionary Society, the Presbyterians, the Friends, and the Africa Inland Mission had gathered, and in the autumn of 1907 I was back in England.

This journey had shewn me, amongst other things, Mohammedanism in South Africa and East Africa, that *miracle of modern missions*—Uganda—and converts from tribes such as Zulus, Massai, and others, thought at that time to be the most warlike in Africa.

Tropical Outfit. I had lived in tents in Egypt, the Libyan desert, Tripoli, Northern Nigeria, and East Africa. Camping out and depending on few extraneous supplies always had for me great attractions. Having made a minute study of matters of tropical outfit for twelve years, preparations for a trans-African journey in the way of camping paraphernalia, food supplies, and clothing were easily made. As wearing apparel and food are very much matters of taste, advice is difficult to give. Personal predilection should be carefully considered. To tell a man that he must take so much jam and so much sauce and so much chocolate on a tour into Central Africa is a very serious responsibility.

"De gustibus non disputandum."

But there are certain general rules it is well to consider. I agree with most other Central African travellers that tinned meats, and especially tinned fish, should be barred. Dried fruit of some half dozen different kinds should certainly be carried, besides a large quantity of milk and easily-digested farinaceous foods.

Woollen underclothes I have found to be a *sine qua non*, especially in the rainy season, when perhaps for days I was unable to get dry.

A TRANS-AFRICAN JOURNEY

I differ from other explorers, such as Rohlfs and Barth, who have maintained that as sheep have no wool in the tropics, wool should not be used as a clothing. Let men take my testimony for what it is worth. Rohlfs and Barth have travelled extensively in and through Central Africa clothed in cotton. They have lived to tell the tale. I have spent years in the same or similar regions wrapped in wool, and am still to-day enjoying most excellent health.

A good supply of medicines, bandages, cotton wool and antiseptics, besides tooth forceps and certain other surgical instruments, I found useful. A few of my medicines that were sent after me never reached me; amongst them *oil of citronella*, which seems to be the only patent medicine that frightens away mosquitoes. A good supply of this oil will confer a great boon on the traveller during the evening hours.

Three specialities of outfit which I made use of in Central Africa I desire to recommend. A waterproof poncho, which is an overcoat, tent, and ground sheet in one. Several of the best camel-hair rugs, which are warm when dry and warmer still when wet, and this in the mountain regions of Central Africa, especially in the rainy season, is a most important matter. A third speciality is boots. Strong long shafted white sealskin boots, with four soles and a few nails, are as light as they are durable, excellent for riding and tramping through the bush. I had several pairs of long boots with me, but practically only wore one of the fore-

[margin: Poncho, Camel-hair Rugs and Sealskin Boots.]

mentioned pairs. I must have marched somewhat over three thousand miles in them, and only the fourth sole was gone.

Certain other things which I did not find a success included dried milk, which would not mix after six months in the tropics. The American wooden army saddle (cowboy) gives the African barb easily a sore back. Pith helmets are a nuisance. They get squashed when packed, and become pulp when wet. If anybody could invent a suitable sunproof headgear, the blessing of all white Central Africans would be his sure reward.

Camp Furniture. The French Government Tonnelet made of corrugated iron, water and air tight, and easily opened, is the most useful packing case I know of for Central Africa. X furniture is too weak for tours that extend over a year or more, but is to-day practically the only handy thing at our disposal, as bed, chair, table, bath, washstand and stool, all go into one *soit disant* waterproof bag.

The tent should be large enough to hold, besides the bed and boxes, a table and chair, so that the traveller could have his meals in the tent if it rains. A tent ten feet by eight, with a double roof, should have an outer sheet projecting all round and thus give protection to the loads stored under it.

Canoes. Two collapsible Canadian canoes weighing twenty pounds each, with four paddles, would take away all the terrors of swollen rivers, as they might be tied together to form a stable raft.

I had only one of these canoes with me, and this was too frail an affair for some of the great streams.

Had I had two, instead of hanging about the banks of the Kotto river for five days, I would have gone across in an hour or two with my caravan.

Books are a great boon in Central Africa, **Mental** and at one time or other, on my Central **Food.** African journeys, I read through most of the English classics. The monotony of a daily march or ride of from six to eight hours becomes unbearable if the mind is allowed to wander. The lack of regular reading is the cause of much of the mental trouble of the white man in the tropics. Quite a number of travellers and Government men, and even missionaries, have gone out of their minds through brooding over their own thoughts. They usually begin with misunderstandings, then come mis-representations, and at last the cockatrice's egg is hatched out into lunacy.

There is no difficulty about carrying crockery nowadays in Central Africa. If the boys are good they are far more careful than servants at home, and of the set of crockery I took into Central Africa by way of the Niger, only those pieces that I myself had broken had disappeared when I reached the Nile. Food eaten from tin tastes tinny, and as vegetables are usually wooden and the meat tough, the meals are not appetising, and unless a white table cloth, a clean serviette and white crockery, with certain attractive condiments are at one's disposal to make one's meals a little more tempting, the food is apt to be taken away from the table in the same way as it is placed upon it. The old saying,

"Mens sana in corpore sano,"

Spiritual and Mental Health. is a proverb oftentimes misunderstood, but essentially true. Spiritual holiness hardly dwells in the demented, and perfect mental balance and penetration is in the majority of cases closely linked with physical health. There seems to be no reason why the spiritual life of a man should suffer in the lonely wilds of tropical Central Africa. Jesus Christ used to go into the wilderness by Himself to pray, and His most favourite time for prayer was the night. In darkness and loneliness He had communion with the Father. In practising the presence of God we are independent of our fellowmen. So far from being a hindrance to the development of spiritual life, the lonely wilderness should be the very training ground for it.

Why then is it that Professor Drummond, when out in British Central Africa, asked his companion to separate from him, as he did not desire to lose his friendship, and he realised his shortening temper and lack of spirituality would eventually result in his falling out with his friend? *This is a common experience of most devoted missionaries and Christian people in Central Africa.* It seems pitiful that it should be so, but it is advisable to recognise the fact at the outset.

A TRANS-AFRICAN JOURNEY

I therefore determined to attempt the crossing of the Continent from the Niger to the Nile alone; and while taking first one of my fellow-labourers as far as German Adamawa, and then German and French officials over part of the road, the most dangerous districts I traversed alone.

From the human standpoint it was very probable that the attempted traverse of Africa would remain an attempt. If it is to-day an accomplished fact, it is simply that God has seen fit to use an instrument, which, however well-fitted it might have been in physical training, was certainly utterly inadequate to accomplish what it essayed to do. And it is only in the realisation that nothing happens apart from His direction or permission, that I find an explanation for the simplicity with which obstacles were overcome and dangers disappeared.

God's time has come that the tribes in the heart of the Continent should be won for the Christian faith; that the last babies of our British Empire who, from the nurseries of Northern Nigeria and the Anglo-Egyptian Sudan, are stretching out their hands to us, should be saved from the baneful consequences and the blight which would fall upon these lands should Islam succeed in its threatened conquest. **God's Time has Come.**

Ethiopia is stretching out her hands unto God; Christ is stretching out His hands to Ethiopia, to His little ones; and we, as followers of Christ, may either join or separate, may either raise or repulse. For the first time in the history of

Central Africa we may put the out-stretched hands of the sons of midnight, out-stretched from the heart of the Dark Continent, into the out-stretched hands of the Christ, the Light of the World.

A Lesson in Geography, and A Visit to the Sudan United Mission Stations

> "We are used to public compliments and private indifference. We are treated as people who must belong to the human race, but who cannot be recognised as brothers and friends."
>
> *Dr. Horton (speaking for the negroes).*

CHAPTER III

"I SAY, Dr. Kumm, you have been telling us a good deal about the Sudan—the Sudan! See, the Sudan is in Egypt, is it not?"

See! The Sudan is in Egypt?

A white-haired gentleman questioned me after an hour's address on the crisis in Africa. It had been stated that it was further from the Capital of the Western Sudan to the Capital of the Eastern Sudan, or from Timbuktu to Khartum, than from London to Timbuktu. It had been reaffirmed that the Sudan was larger than China proper, larger than the whole of Europe minus Russia, and the question—"See, the Sudan is in Egypt?"—was not a little disconcerting. Egypt is well-known to all of us—many of us have been there, seen its monuments, heard of its mysteries. We know that Egypt consists of nothing but the narrow Nile Valley, some 700 miles in length, and at its widest four to five miles across, plus the Nile Delta, which is about the size of Holland. The Anglo-Egyptian Sudan alone is some twenty times as large as Egypt; and the Anglo-Egyptian Sudan is only about one-third of the whole Sudan.

Is Lake Chad near Uganda?

Questions a saintly lady after another lecture: " Please tell me, Dr. Kumm, is Lake Chad somewhere near Uganda ? "

Hesitatingly I answer, " Well, no, not exactly. True, it is not very far according to American ideas; it is a considerable distance according to British ideas; about three times as far as from the Channel to John o' Groat's. But, according to African ideas, it is very far indeed."

I had the privilege of travelling last year (1909) from the Lake Chad region to Uganda, and doing this either on horseback or on foot, I realised that the distance was quite a respectable one.

At the same meeting another lady asked, " You get to the Shari by going up the Zambesi, do you not ? "

The Shari and The Shire.

Answer: "No, your Ladyship. Going up the Zambesi one comes to the Shire. I was speaking about the Shari, a river navigable in the rainy season for some 700 miles, which flows into Lake Chad, and forms one of the six great river systems of Africa."

Mr. Mott's latest book containing missionary statistics says there are twenty-seven million Pagans or Mohammedans in the interior of Asia unreached to-day by Christian Missions, and some seventy million Pagans and Moslems in Africa, also not reached by our modern missionary enterprise. The latter figure, I would think, is overestimated. If one divides Africa politically, the following great Protectorates are untouched by Protestant Missions:—

A LESSON IN GEOGRAPHY

(*a*) The French Western Sudan, with its Capital, Timbuktu.

(*b*) The British Lake Chad region (the Sultanate of Bornu).

(*c*) The German Lake Chad region; German Bornu and Adamawa.

(*d*) The French Shari Chad Protectorate.

(*e*) The French Sahara.

(*f*) Turkish Fezzan.

(*g*) The Anglo-Egyptian Sudan West of the Nile.

(*h*) The districts round Nyangwe on the Lualaba (Belgian Congo), and the South-Western parts of that same Colony.

(*i*) The greater part of the Portuguese Colonies.

Unreached by Protestant Missions.

From the orographical standpoint, three-quarters of the North-Central African ironstone plateau is unoccupied by Protestant Missions. This plateau region is fairly healthy, and cannot be compared for a moment with the gallery forest districts of the Zambesi, the Congo, or the Lower Niger.

The Central African Ironstone Plateau.

The Sudan is situated south of the Sahara, and stretches across the greatest width of Africa.

There may be in the Sudan a population of from thirty to forty millions.

The statistics used by me up to the present were taken from the Statesman's Year Book, from Stanford's "Geography of Africa," and other standard works, but I find all the figures given in them for the Sudan considerably in excess of the real facts, and the following compilation would seem to me more correct:—

There are 8 million people in Northern Nigeria.
Perhaps 10 million in the hinterland of West Africa, the French Western Sudan.
3 or 4 million in German Adamawa and Bornu.
7 million in the Mobangi-Shari-Chad Protectorate.
2 million in the Anglo-Egyptian Sudan.

Total 30 million.

Of these, some twenty million are still Pagan, and if one reckons for each Protestant missionary in the Sudan—and there are about fifty—a population of a hundred thousand people, that leaves twenty-five million without a preacher of the Gospel. Thus is the Sudan the greatest unevangelised territory, with the greatest number of people that have not yet been reached by the Gospel. There may be another ten to fifteen million in Africa in the fore-mentioned parts outside the Sudan, bringing the unreached population of Africa to thirty-five or forty million. Of these forty million, some fifteen to eighteen million are Mohammedans and about twenty-five million Pagans. It is these latter twenty-five million that Mohammedanism threatens to win for the Crescent faith.

An Expedition of Investigation. In order to study the success of the Moslem propaganda in Central Africa more adequately, I traversed the Continent last year, after having visited the Mission Stations of the Sudan United Mission, following roughly the border lines

A LESSON IN GEOGRAPHY 37

between Mohammedanism and Paganism in the Sudan. In the next pages I will endeavour to give a short outline* of my journey that may be of interest to the reader.

The Governments of Great Britain, France, and Germany had done everything they could to assist in this journey of investigation. Two letters are subjoined, one from the Colonial Minister in Paris and the other from the Secretary to the Administration in Northern Nigeria, addressed to the various residents in that Protectorate. *[Government Assistance.]*

République Française,
Liberté—Egalité—Fraternité,
Paris, le 6th Oct, 1908.

[Letter of Recommendation from French Colonial Office.]

Ministère des Colonies Direction des Affaires Politiques et Administratives, Sous-Direction de l'Afrique et Service Géographique et des Missions.

Voyage d'études de M. le Docteur Kumm :

Le Ministre de l'Instruction Publique et des Beaux-Arts, chargé de l'intérim de Ministère des Colonies, à Monsieur le Gouverneur Général de l'Afrique Occidentale française.

M. le Docteur Kumm, connu par ses travaux relatifs à la Nubie, l'Adamaoua et la Nigéria septentrionale, qui vous remettra la présente lettre, entreprend un voyage d'études du Niger au Nil, en vue de compléter les connaissances qu'il possède sur les divers états du Soudan, en

---

* More elaborate geographical information will be found in my previous book, "From Hausaland to Egypt through the Sudan."

visitant à nouveau le Bagirmi, le Oudaï méridional et le Bahr el Gasahl.

J'ai l'honneur de vous prier de vouloir bien lui faciliter, dans la mesure du possible, les moyens de poursuivre les travaux qu'il a entrepris, et je vous serai obligé de le recommander, dans ce but, au bon accueil des autorités locales placées sous votre haute administration.

October 12, 1908. (Signed) GASTON.

From the Secretary to the Administration of Northern Africa to the Resident, Bornu Province.

Dr. Karl Kumm, Secretary of the Sudan United Mission, has come out from England on a tour of inspection, and to settle several important matters with His Excellency in connection with the Mission, including that of taking over Freed Slaves from the Home at Zunguru for the Lucy Memorial Home at Rumasha, Nassarawa Province. Dr. Kumm may have occasion to visit your Province, in which case I am directed by His Excellency to request that you will afford him every facility and assistance.

(Signed) M. H. D. BERESFORD,
Secretary.

The Secretariat, Zunguru, 12th November, 1908.

(Copy of letter addressed to the various Residents in Northern Nigeria.)

The German Government also had written to their officials in Garua and Kusseri, and these did their best. Everything combined to diminish difficulties and obstacles that had to be expected.

A LESSON IN GEOGRAPHY

In the Niger Territories.

The journey in the Niger Territories, of course, was a pleasure. The country had much changed since my visit in 1904. Lokoja could hardly be recognised. Great engineering shops and a foundry had been erected by Government, a landing-stage, roads and streets with clean ditches and shady avenues looked very different from the narrow paths, overgrown by rank grass, which I had found there on my former visit. Several new trading firms had been established; the Church Missionary Society had built a new Mission House, the Government had erected a large splendid church; but the old bungalow in which the first mission party of the Sudan United Mission had camped on arriving in Northern Nigeria was still there, and I made use of it again.

The population of Lokoja is increasing continually. There is no doubt that Lokoja is the natural capital for Northern and Southern Nigeria.

The marine superintendent, Captain Elliott, informed me on my arrival that His Excellency the Governor desired me, if I could conveniently do so, to come up immediately to Zunguru, as he expected shortly to go north and visit the great Mohammedan cities. The largest boat in Northern Nigeria, the "Corona," had been kept waiting for me—at least, so I was given to understand—in order that I might join her. Twice I had to tranship as I ascended the river up country.

At Baro, the starting point of the Baro-Kano

Up the Kaduna.

Railway, I transhipped from the "Corona" to a smaller steamer, in which I continued as far as Mureji. Here I left the Niger and the steamers and descended into a dug-out, as the Kaduna did not carry water enough to float even the smallest steamer. A number of officers who were going up to Zunguru for their Hausa examinations had arrived at Mureji by the same boat, but took things a little more leisurely, and I passed them on returning from Zunguru, having spent three days there. I was not a little proud, having broken the poling record up the Kaduna. Eighty-four miles in two days against a strong current is not bad work. The polers were greatly delighted with their *dash* of two sheep besides the pay.

The last twenty-two miles from Barejuko to Zunguru were traversed luxuriously in a steam-tram. In this same steam-tram, too, things had been improved since my last visit. In 1904 there were only cattle-trucks, into which Sir William Wallace and other Government men who took me up country placed their camp chairs. This time there were first and third class cars, with uniformed officials. On first arriving in Barejuko on this journey the steam-tram could not be found. There was nobody at the station except a watchman, and yet it was ten o'clock in the morning.

I enquired from the gentleman what time the tram would arrive, and was told that there would be no tram that day.

"Why not?"

"Ba-nji-ba" (I do not know).

From the railway station I went to the telegraph office, but in the telegraph office, too, there seemed to be a holiday. A clerk, when asked why the Government offices were closed, informed me in a very superior, graciously condescending way, that to-day was the King's birthday, and so indeed it was. After a short palaver I was permitted to send a telegram to the Governor informing him of my arrival at Barejuko, and shortly after an answer came back. **Barejuko.** His Excellency was sorry that the tram had not been sent down that day. Would I come up to Zunguru by it next morning.

A number of good mud houses and some well-cleared ground constituted a very desirable camping place, and when later on another European appeared, who happened to know some friends of mine at Clonskeagh Castle, Dublin, the hours of the day were spent very pleasantly. This good man had come to get money to pay his workmen. He led the vanguard building gangs of the new Lagos-Kano railroad.

On the 10th of November, 1908, I arrived **At Zunguru** at Zunguru. The hospitality shown me by His Excellency the Governor was of the kindest. Sir Percy Girouard is a man with a considerable reserve force, and also a good deal of *arrière pensée*, essentially a strong man.

In the evenings' conversation on the verandah of Government House he used to draw out some of those present who were anxious to agree with their superior's statements. Sir Percy would, for example, say, " Drunkenness is a very bad vice." "Yes, sir," would chime in somebody, "These people here at Zunguru are an awfully drunken crowd," thinking that he was following up his chief's cue in the right way, when suddenly His Excellency would turn on him with —"You make there a very strong statement. What reason have you for saying what you have just said? When did you see the last drunken man or woman in this place?" In vain did our friend try to modify his statement. He was told that he had no business to make a statement that he could not prove.

Zunguru, too, had developed considerably during the four years. A new irrigation farm had just been laid out, and a couple of Egyptian *shadufs* supplied the water. The prison seemed to be the special pride of His Excellency, who himself took me to the various places of interest. The new railway cutting appeared a further development, and last but not least, that which interested me most, the Freed Slaves' Home was more sanitary and more prosperous than formerly.

The West-End of the Wilderness Nearly all the conveniences of civilised life may be had in this West-End of the wilderness. In the morning the soda-water wagon comes round, and the iceman, and when I left, the kind Secretary to the Administration, Mr. De la Poer Beresford, sent a large chunk of ice to keep me cool on the journey in the train.

During my stay at Government House, a number of leases for various Mission Stations of the Sudan United Mission were prepared and signed, and also an Agreement arrived at between His Excellency the Governor, and myself, as to the taking over of the Government freed slaves' children into the proposed Lucy Memorial Home at Rumasha.

The three days in Zunguru were very soon gone, and on the 13th of November I left in a special train Sir Percy had ordered, and commenced my journey back to Lokoja. I had the driver of my special stop at the Wushishi Mission Station for an hour of fellowship and prayer, and then journeyed on, spent a few hours at Baro, and was back in Lokoja five days after my departure from Zunguru.

A party of seven missionaries, a perfect number, had accompanied me to Northern Nigeria to reinforce the staff of the Sudan United Mission. Two of them, Mr. J. L. Maxwell and Mr. J. Young, had been out before, and were returning from their furlough.

Two South Africans had come from the Southland to join as the representatives of that new branch of the Mission in the enterprise against Islam; one of them an Afrikander, and the other a former Y.M.C.A. Secretary of Kimberley, a Britisher. Both had been in the South African war on different sides, but had now become fast friends. Messrs. Botha and Hosking formed an excellent combination, and are worthy representatives of the great new African Dominion. **Members of Mission Party.**

Besides these there were three new men from our little Northland—a medical man, Dr. G. Alexander, from Dublin; Rev. E. Evans, a young minister from Wales; and Mr. Cooper, an evangelist from London. And last but not least, there was Tom, my faithful personal boy, who was going as a worker to the Lucy Memorial Freed Slaves' Home. Our fellowship on board the steamer on our way out had been of the happiest, and longingly we all looked forward to useful work in the Sudan.

It was my intention to visit the various Mission Stations, beginning with the new site for the Freed Slaves' Home at Rumasha; then continue to the Bauchi Hill country to see Bukuru and Ngell; and by way of the C.M.S. Station, Panyam, call at Langtang and Rock Station, Dempar, Ibi, Wukari, and Donga, making in all nine posts of the Sudan United Mission, and one post of the C.M.S. Two of these stations were unoccupied at the time, and have since been given up; *i.e.*, Ngell and Rock Station.

A new outpost far away from the others on the Upper Benué at M'bula has been established, where our South African friends, reinforced by a third new man from the Cape, have begun a promising work. The Stations of the S.U.M. are divided in the following way :—

The Upper Benué District belongs to the South Africans. South of the Benué River are our American friends at Wukari and Donga. The Murchison Range and the Stations on the Middle and Lower Benué are manned by Britishers; and the Freed Slaves' Home is a union enterprise. It is proposed to add to the present Institution, a

A LESSON IN GEOGRAPHY 45

School for the sons of chiefs, and a Seminary for the training of teachers.

To the Freed Slaves' Home I will refer in a future chapter. Let me now give a few incidents of my visits to the stations where missionary work was carried on. *Freed Slaves' Home.*

On the Bukuru Plateau the work, being hardly a year old, was entirely in its initiatory stages, but a few liberated slave boys kept by Dr. Emlyn, and who have since been handed over to Rev. Evans, are being trained and should become useful helpers in the future. Slowly the confidence of the natives is secured.

On the arrival of our missionaries there, the people were as shy as deer, and even to-day they will not come out of their houses after nightfall. These pagans have always been free, and cannot be enslaved. They die of heart failure if their liberty is taken from them. The Chief of Ngell, having made himself objectionable to the Government representative, was taken out of his village and sent as a prisoner to Bauchi, but both he and a companion of his, on their arrival at the Government headquarters, died suddenly without any apparent reason. And every time one of these Kibyen people has been sent out of the country or imprisoned he has died. They are liberty-loving men of the mountains, and, if won for the Christ, will form a strong nucleus of a healthy Christian nation of the future.

Dr. Emlyn desired me to make known that there was work for fifty missionaries in the Bauchi hill country, but at the present moment *Dr. Emlyn's Request.*

there are only five there. Since tin has been found on the plateau, numbers of European mining engineers have made themselves at home in the healthy highlands, and Mohammedan traders and Mohammedan workmen are invading the territories of the mountain tribes, inaccessible to them but a short time ago on account of the standing feud between the fetish worshippers and the Moslems.

TRIBES OF THE BAUCHI HILL COUNTRY.

BURUM TRIBE.

Afang	1088	souls.
Assob	2436	,,
Bukuru	10434	,,
Ding	656	,,
Forum	10740	,,
Gashish	60	,,
Hepan	2917	,,
Hoss	5036	,,
Tor	2376	,,
Kassa	2385	,,
Kuru	3510	,,
Kiri	450	,,
Machi	1420	,,
Ngell	5400	,,
Ngwarra	48	,,
Rafam	2616	,,
Talom	430	,,
Rim	3399	,,
Riom	810	,,
Rop	2148	,,
Sho	1104	,,
Tafam	2690	,,
Vom	11974	,,
Waran	1180	,,
Oshono	1200	,,
Total	76507	souls.

RUKABA TRIBE.

Achaka	4783	souls.
Balsa	2832	,,
Robo	1116	,,
Zamagan	2989	,,
Total	11720	souls.

BARON TRIBE.

Batura, etc.	9876	souls.

SURA TRIBE.

Panyam	5820	souls.
Vodni	4080	,,
Rup	1040	,,
Kumbul	3905	,,
Kereng	3943	,,
Ampam	2989	,,
Mongun	2818	,,
Total	24595	souls.

NAMBURA TRIBE.

Buji	2756	souls.
Guwam	780	,,
Gussam	1488	,,
Jengre	4740	,,
Total	9764	souls.

A LESSON IN GEOGRAPHY

JARAWA.			IRRIGWE.		
Joss, etc. ...	19862	souls.	Kwall Miango	9234	souls.
SANGAWA.			BA.		
Limero ...	1130	souls.	Anobissa ...	4020	souls.
ANAGUTA.			Amokassa...	1548	,,
Naraguta ...	5352	souls.	Limeron ...	960	,,
			Euchari ...	1092	,,
PACHERA.					
Teria ...	1596	souls.	Total ...	7620	souls.

GENERAL SURVEY OF THE PRECEDING.

Burum	Tribe.	Total	...	...	76507	souls.
Rukaba	,,	,,	...	...	11720	,,
Baron	,,	,,	...	...	9826	,,
Sura	,,	,,	...	...	24595	,,
Nambura	,,	,,	...	...	9764	,,
Jarawa	,,	,,	...	...	19862	,,
Sangawa	,,	,,	...	...	1130	,,
Anaguta	,,	,,	...	...	5352	,,
Pachera	,,	,,	...	...	1596	,,
Irrigwe	,,	,,	...	...	9234	,,
Ba	,,	,,	...	...	7620	,,
		Grand Total	...	...	177206	,,

LIST OF PAGAN TRIBES AND POPULATIONS IN BAUCHI PROVINCE.

Deinawa	...	...	5434	Zegi Zegi	...	...	4508
Gerawa	...	...	9347	Girmawa	...	...	3607
Seiawa	...	...	15660	Kubawa	...	...	690
Jarawa	...	...	19862	Barawa	...	...	2071
Shirawa	...	...	12310	Barawan Dutse	...	1848
Bankalawa	...	...	9685	Pyemawa	...	...	3363
Beilawa	...	...	1901	Sigiddiawa	...	...	864
Bolewa	...	...	6541	Yanyamawa	...	...	1240
Larabawa	...	...	1073	Galambawa	...	...	1629

Angassawa (Plain)	27826	Sirawa		221
Ajawa	330	Kaniya Wuro		83
Berkawa	377	Kariya Wadafa		178
Zarawa	322	Daniilawa		403
Zulawa	565	Kuriya Gidda		293
Burmawa	76507	Mujawa		2527
Warjawa	864	Ganisawa		202
Jimbimawa	155	Munawa		350
Dajawa	508	Jukimawa		457
Dazawa	85	Dugurawa		272
Fawa	74	Shengawa		192
Sagawa	160	Tula Tangale		30035
Koptawa	106	Waja		11983
Boyawa	359	Angassawa (Hill)		53000
Femawa	396	Surawa and Baron		40000
Bajamawa	641	Dass District		10000
Zaranda (Habe)	1210	Ningi		25000
Gingimawa	3200	Rukaba		11720
Zakshi Habe	1027	Nambura		9764
Goberawa	600	Sangawa		1130
Kerawa	324	Anaguta		5252
Bamborro	2114	Pachera		1596
Zanawa	246	Irrigwe		9234
Kirr	443	Ba		7620
Jimawa	412			
		Total		441,996

Langtang, the next district of the Sudan United Mission, is situated at the foot of the Murchison Range. A new bungalow is built on a *Juju-hill*, where once human sacrifices were wont to be made periodically. Several tribes live around Langtang Station. Behind it, within five or six miles of the hills, are the Gazum cannibals. To the north-east are the Burmawa, to the west the Montoil, the Girkawa, and the Ankwes. Around the station and on the plain of the Wasé River live the Yergum.

A LESSON IN GEOGRAPHY

Dozens of hamlets, the grass huts closely built together, are hidden away amongst rich, ripe fields of guinea corn. The Yergum and the other tribes, with the exception of the Gazum, have come a little more into contact with the outside world than the Kibyen on the plateau, but most of them are innocent of clothing. The men are tall, lithe, with beautifully-shaped limbs, and very different from the heavy coast negro.

The Yergum.

Amongst the Burmawa, copper-coloured skin and red Indian features are quite common. Stately women, fearsome as antelopes, one frequently meets with along the road.

These people are still very shy, but in their own hamlets in the harvest season, when the world is smiling and there are music and love in the air, many a perfect-shaped Venus and Apollo may be seen creeping out of unexpected hovels to join the evening village ball. They are a bright and happy people, well worth winning for our Christian faith.

Rock Station, where, in September, 1904, the foundations were laid for the first building of the Sudan United Mission, was in ruins.

> "In den oeden Fensterhoelen
> Wohnt das Grauen
> Und des Himmels Wolken schauen
> Hoch hinein."

Since the great fire which destroyed the roof of the building, the place had not been built up again, the original idea of an industrial and educational centre not having proved itself

Rock Station in Ruins.

workable. A solitary watchman lived in one of the remaining huts of the Mission Compound; the weeds and grass and bush grew around the ruined remnants of the house. How quickly prolific nature in the Tropics covers up decay.

I remembered the happy, hopeful days of early sowing and building in Pioneer Camp at Rock Station, and it was almost with regret that I looked upon the present dilapidation; but remembering the law of life, that no growth is possible unless old garments are shed whenever they become unsuitable or too small, I would not take one solitary man from the districts occupied at the present moment to reopen Rock Station. On sentimental grounds one could not but be sad, but in a practical matter of fact way one was bound to rejoice.

The next station, and the last before Ibi with the coming Conference, was Dempar. The carriers accompanying me had by this time been sifted, and were carefully chosen men; and to put their endurance to the test with the view of finding out their stability for a Trans-African journey, I let them march in one day from Rock Station to Dogon-kurmi, a distance of some thirty-two or thirty-five miles. There was no difficulty. None lagged behind, and though we only got into camp about nine o'clock in the evening on a moonless night, all were cheerful and pleased with the success of the trial march.

At Dempar. Next day early we arrived at Dempar. I had heard so much about the very promising work on

A LESSON IN GEOGRAPHY

this Benué River Station that I looked forward to meeting with Mr. and Mrs. Burt, who were at that time in charge. The Chief, who was an old friend, the Chief's son, who had been with us at Pioneer Camp, and one of the elders of the village, a hunter named Dogeri, were well-known faces.

Dogeri's only child, a little boy of four years of age, had been brought to me at Rock Station by two men.

"Whose is this child?" I asked.

Answer: "The child is yours."

Writer: "Mine! What do you mean?"

Answer: "The child belongs to Dogeri, and you blessed it four years ago after it was born, and prayed the great God to bless it and make it a blessing. Are you not, therefore, its father?"

At Dempar there was a very flourishing Day School, a Sunday School, and a Sunday service attended regularly by the Chief and a considerable number of his people.

And now for the Ibi Conference. Forty miles down the Benué, and the dug-out canoes ground on the Ibi beach.

Ibi had changed too. Instead of one factory of the Niger Company, there were three; instead of the one house of the Resident on the ridge behind the town, there was a whole hamlet of bungalows. The market place was busier than ever. The Chief's house had grown in size, as he had evidently grown in importance. A chief mosque had been built, and the evening call to prayer came from different parts of the town.

Ibi Conference.

Things had changed indeed in Ibi in four years' time. The Jukun village had become a Moslem Hausa trade centre.

Fourteen missionaries from various stations had come together to discuss methods of work, the administration of the Mission in the Field, and further development.

The Ibi Conference was remarkable in more senses than one. It was the first Missionary Conference in the Sudan, east or west. It was a Conference held on the banks of "The Mother of Waters" (Benué), some three hundred miles up river, where up to 1904 no missionary had ever preached the Gospel of Jesus Christ. This district (Ibi Dempar District) was the farthest outpost inland in the Central Sudan. To the east it was more than fifteen hundred miles, as the crow flies (not that it is likely that a crow would fly as far), to the nearest Mission Station on the Nile; to the north more than two thousand miles to the first Christian witness in Tripoli on the Mediterranean.

In the centre of the native town we formed a compound, a combination of several native enclosures which we rented from the people, and here our meetings were held. A rudimentary mosque was handed over to us by a Mohammedan for our meeting place.

A large wild fig tree stretched its branches over Mohammed's mosque, which had now become a Christian meeting house. True, its walls consisted only of grass matting, and the roof was nothing but three layers of similar mats, yet it was

A LESSON IN GEOGRAPHY

private, and it served its purpose. Several tents were pitched, and two or three houses taken possession of by our friends from Dempar and Langtang, Wukari and Donga, besides the new Mission party. The only absentees were Dr. Emlyn on the Bukuru Plateau and Mr. Martin at Rumasha.

Our Sunday morning service, attended by the Resident, the white officers, and the coloured clerks from the coast, representing the Christian community of Ibi, was the first Christian fellowship meeting held at that place, and the evening evangelistic lantern service, also attended by several of the white officials and a considerable crowd of Ibians, was quite a success. With a Communion service our Conference closed.

Small and insignificant it was from the human standpoint, yet charged with large possibilities for the future, announcing with its feeble voice the initiation of the evangelisation of the largest unreached Mission Field of to-day.

A further visit to our American Stations, Wukari and Donga, was as pleasant as it was instructive. The work of the Rev. G. W. Guinter, at Wukari, has the mark of permanency: his influence is felt in the town, he is respected and loved by many of the natives.

Two promising schools, one in each of the two centres, have in them the elements of stability, and should do much to shape the future of the Jukun district.

This part of the Mission Field, like many other fields in the world, is undermanned.

Last year saw no fewer than twenty-five University men in the United States killed in games of football. These twenty-five men, imbued with the spirit of Jesus Christ, changed from nominal Christians to true followers of the Christ, would have made a vast difference in the Sudan, had they given their lives for the good of these nations.

Twenty-five young men killed by football!

What has Jesus Christ, what has even commonsense to say to such cheap sacrifice of life?

A Day's Work

"The Lantern-bearer does not see the Road before him."

CHAPTER IV

"BATURE, Bature." "White Man! White Man!" A final stretch, and I attempt to turn over, and in turning over, turn out. The gray dawn is just beginning to light up the tent, though there is only a shade of difference between the night and the morning. Stiffly I climb into my riding gear, pull on my boots, and stumble out of the tent. One of the boys has in the meantime put up a chair and a table that were folded and packed away for the night.

A thunder whistle sounds through the camp. The cook sits up yawning, warming himself over the embers of last night's fire, and then begins to poke it up to make tea. A second sounding of the whistle, and the headmen straggle up from their fires to pull down the tent. Two of the boys are busy rolling up the bed, hauling out the boxes and locking them. My instrument bag is brought, thermometer, barometer, wind and rain gauge noted down. Tea is ready; the horse stands saddled. A third sounding of the whistle, and while I am munching a biscuit and enjoying a warm cup of *water bewitched*, the carriers are doing up their loads; the teapot, cup and saucer disappear in the

Turn over? Turn out!

The Start. crockery box, and just when the sun begins to peep over the horizon the trek begins.

"*Ku dauka kaiya*" (take up the loads).

Three native elephant hunters, the path-finders of the caravan, each with a hatchet, dive into the long grass, sopping wet with the morning dew, taking their direction towards the rising sun. The grass is, on an average, ten feet high. The first man with his hands stretched out in front opens the way, the two behind him trample down the grass.

Then follow a couple of headmen and soldiers with matchets. The path becomes three feet wide.

After the soldiers, the first carrier with a load, *Giwa* (the "Elephant.").

And then the long line of carriers, the oxen and horses, goats and sheep, the Mecca pilgrims, more headmen, and lastly myself, mounted on a slow, heavy pony.

The many men passing through the grass have shaken the damp dew from the sharp blades of the reeds and the rank vegetation. Yet the waterproof apron covering the knees of the traveller is soaked through within ten minutes of the start.

French traders usually wear thin blue or white cotton pantaloons. These get wet very easily, but also dry again quickly when the sun comes out, and there is something to be said for these garments. Heavy riding breeches look more respectable, and with snakes and scorpions around are safer if one sits down on the ground,

A DAY'S WORK

One of the headmen starts a song, to this effect.

"We have come from a far-off land, and we are going to the rising Sun."

He repeats this twice, and then all the carriers join in and repeat it twice.

Merry Music.

The previous soloist continues.

"We have plenty of meat to eat, and we do not fear the hungry bush."

And again the echo from the men.

"Our white father's name is Madugu. He gives us plenty to eat."

And so on, *da capo al fine*.

The men are at their best. Two hours' march, and the long, swinging strides have taken us over the first seven miles. The bush opens a little, the grass becomes thinner, rocks appear, the place seems suitable for ten minutes' rest.

A shrill call from the whistle of the chief headman who is just in front of me. The signal is taken up and answered by the first sub-headman of the line, perhaps a quarter of a mile in front; and the snake-like line of the caravan is rolled up and comes to rest on an open stony slope. A few of the loads want re-roping, one or two sore feet are bandaged, the men stretch themselves, one or two get out their stumpy pipes for a whiff of tobacco. The girth of the white man's horse is tightened; I mount, and on this second lap of the march take the lead.

The two or three war-boys, on whom the French Government insisted, move to the tail-end of the caravan. With only one hunter in front, I canter ahead, rifle in hand. The grass is getting dry, and there is a chance of meeting with game.

Mile after mile is left behind. Accompanied by only two men, I am a thousand yards ahead of the rest of the men, when the leading hunter stops short. One foot in the air like a perfect pointer, his hands and arms do not move, but his eyes are glued to a little open space on the right.

Shooting for the pot. Silently I glide to the ground. The second hunter has the horse by the reins. Three hartebeest are quietly feeding less than a hundred and fifty yards away. The horse paws the ground, lifts up its nostrils, and neighs. Like lightning, the horned heads of the hartebeest swing round. They gaze intently. If there is to be meat in camp, it is time to fire; and a soft-nosed bullet speeds on its way. With the sound of the shot, there is a three-fold leap into the grass, and the game has disappeared, but not before one of them, the biggest buck, has by a twist of its body and a high kick of its hind heel marked a lung-shot. Quickly I mount, and the horse goes full tilt for the place where the wounded antelope has gone to shelter. But the grass is high. Shall we ever see the wounded game again?

Yes, there it is! The horse stands still, pulled up suddenly. The buck, not more than ten yards away, looks for a moment at me. But this moment is just half a moment too long. Crack! and shot through the heart the buck sinks to the ground. With long leaps and a shout the two hunters are soon on the scene. The caravan comes up, rests a quarter of an hour, and by that time the venison has been divided into chunks of, roughly, five to ten pounds each; the skin, head, and horns are rolled up and tied to one of the loads.

"*Ku dauka kaiya,*" and the march continues. Twenty minutes, and a mighty stampede to the left tells of big game. A herd of buffaloes has been strolling slowly across the path in front, but with the wind in their favour, they scented the caravan and now are careering away, kicking up no end of dust.

The roughly blazed trail, blazed by the vanguard which is a day or two in front to lay out our camping-grounds from day to day, follows a freshly-made elephant track. The ground is soft after yesterday's rain, and the deep holes made by the feet of the giant pachyderms are half full of water, and riding becomes almost impossible. The carriers slither and slide about; the loads slip off the heads of the men into the yellow mud. Labourers at home would use bad language, but my boys in Africa either struggle doggedly along, or laugh at each other's misfortunes. **Elephant Paths.**

We come to a river waist-deep. The pathfinders have gone on without stopping, and the carriers follow, some of them up to their necks in water. They march straight through. Another rise in the ground, another halt.

It is midday. The vertical rays of the sun dry the perspiration on our faces and arms. The brown-black skins of the people that shone and glistened in the morning dew have become dull and grayish. The song of the early morning has long ceased. We have some eighteen miles behind us.

Half an hour's rest, and at 12.30 the line is formed again, the loads are taken up a little more slowly than the last time, but there is no halting and no complaint.

The march, which in the morning was at the rate of three and a half to four miles an hour, has now gone down to two and a half. My horse is perspiring heavily, and our throats are "good and dry." Happily the road leads down hill.

The camping-ground cannot be far away. Two miles more, and at 1.30 we are face to face with a swamp. The guides are ploughing through it, walking on the roots of willows and mangroves that grow in it, when one of them misses his foothold and goes down into the green oozing mud. But the other guides make a dash for him, and just when his hand is disappearing, get hold of it and haul him out again, *still smiling*.

Green oozing mud.

In vain we look for a way round the swamp. There is no way. The men manage to clamber laboriously over fallen trunks of trees, and through the reeds, and safely reach the other side without losing a load.

But what to do with the animals is a problem. A horse is tried first, and goes down up to its neck. Valiantly three men hang on to it, and by main force haul it out again. It is two o'clock. We have tried to the north, and we have tried to the south, but there seems to be no way, when

one of the men comes up with the information that he has found a place a little distance away where the deep mud is only six feet wide, and a bank of earth and mouldering trees runs to the very edge of the deep part. The animals can jump this, and land in three feet of water where the bottom is firm. His information proved to be correct, and at 2.30 all were across.

But in vain we look for a continuation of the blazed trail. A shady valley leads towards the east, and a number of buffalo and elephant paths wind their way in and out amongst the bushes, but there are no blazed trees. Several men go northward along the bank of the swamp, looking for the continuation of our vanguard signs, but there are none. I myself climb up a little knoll, covered with exceptionally long, rank grass, towards an isolated tall tree, when to my astonishment I step out of the grass into the open clearing of the roughly prepared camp. There are two large huts, a little heap of dried sticks, and a clearing fifty yards by fifty. The ground is dry, close to the water, with a large shady tree—an ideal camping-place.

Camp at last.

The day's work is over. Twenty men pitch the tent, twenty men go for wood, twenty men carry water, twenty men build grass shelters, and twenty men cut grass for the animals, while others make themselves useful in cleaning the ground. A cold fowl, a piece of dry bread, and a long drink out of the water-bottle form a most delicious luncheon. The deck chair is placed in the shade of the tree, and half an hour's siesta indulged in, while forty or fifty camp fires begin to flare up.

The meat of the morning is roasted; porridge steams in pots and pans, and sweet is the rest in the warmth of the afternoon.

Evening bag.
At four o'clock, when the sun is half-down to the west, the antelopes come out of the bush into the open fadamas (meadows by brooks, and swamps and rivers), and the guinea-fowl and the bush-fowl begin to call, it is time to see whether more meat for the next day cannot be secured, and with good fortune two partridges, three guinea fowl, and two antelopes are the bag of the evening.

"The day is far spent; the night is at hand," when we return to the tent. Here a steaming hot bath has been got ready by the boys, and after it, a dinner of soup, meat and vegetables, omelette, stewed fruit, and black coffee is well earned and much enjoyed.

Round the Camp fire.
Night has fallen. The giant-sized pale moon has risen like a milk-white disc above the horizon. The cries of the night owl, the leopard, the hyena, and lion are abroad in the bush. The ghostlike shadows of the trees' dense foliage play on the roof of the tent, and on the open spaces among the camp fires. Between the tent and the dining-hut a large pile of wood has been set alight, and its genial warmth is most agreeable in the cool of the evening. The forty or fifty grass shelters, each with its fire in front, give our camp the appearance of a new-born village in the wilderness.

A DAY'S WORK

Some of the older Fulanis and Hausas come sidling up and inform me that they wish to salute me and greet me after the day's toil is over. They look communicative, and so I desire them to sit down, warm themselves, and tell me a little about their country and their lives in the homeland. A number of brilliant stars glitter in the heavens. The Ursa Major has culminated when the chief speaker of my gentlemen in black commences the last of his tales.

The story of the *Sabaa banaht wa sabaa aulahd*.

"You know, white man, all the stars have names, and there are many, many stories told by the old and wise about these souls in the heavens, for each star is a human soul.

Once upon a time.

"Once upon a time there was a great king who lived in abounding wealth in a rich land. His people were happy. He was supremely so, for had he not seven daughters, the most beautiful maidens the sun had ever shone upon.

"About that time an evil beast, a mighty dragon, stronger than a herd of elephants, longer than the longest camel caravan, came from the desert into the country of the great, good king, and began to prey upon the inhabitants. Morning and night it lay in wait for the people as they went into the fields, and out to the farms, and day by day and night by night men, women, and children did not return to their homely huts, for the dragon of the desert had devoured them.

"At last things came to such a pass that there was not a family in the kingdom that had not lost some dear one. There was mourning and wailing and weeping in the land, and the people did not dare to leave their walled towns and villages. The king, beloved by his people, was willing to give his life for his subjects. Old as he was, he prepared to fight the demon of the wilderness. But he dared not leave his seven daughters unprotected. What could he do? What should he do?

"When, lo and behold! one morning, after a sleepless night, he saw seven princes ride towards his royal castle, all mounted on magnificently caparisoned steeds. A fanfare sounded by the trumpeter cantering ahead of them brought the warden of the gate in great speed to the enfiladed entrance.

Princes from a far country.

"'My masters, the seven princes, desire speech of the king of this happy land.'

"'Call not this land happy,' replied the old, white-bearded warden, 'for we are harassed to the very edge of our lives by a most powerful dragon.'

"'There is no fear in my princes of demons or dragons, but they would have speech with thy lord.'

"Slowly the bolts were drawn, the portcullis was opened, the heavy-hinged iron-barred portals swung back, and the grief-stricken aged father of the land appeared.

"'Welcome, children, whence and what news?'

"'The fame of thy beauteous daughters has travelled far through the world, and has come to the land of thy servants thou seest before thee. Fame says that there are none like unto them under the sun, and we have come to ask for their hands.'

"'Ask not for marriage or for wedding feasts, while all the land is plunged in deepest sorrow. But gladly do I welcome you. Brave as your faces, and your steel-sheathed bodies, is the well-earned renown that is speeding ahead of you. Your deeds of valour and your noble exploits have become proverbial in the lists. Come and be welcome to my home and hall.'*

"So the princes entered, a feast ensued, and seven weddings. Around the royal palace, built on the highest hill, seven lesser mounds were crowned with seven forts. And in those forts lived seven happy pairs. Twelve months went by, and at each princely fort a princeling opened his eyes to the world.

<small>Seven Weddings.</small>

"Spring, summer, autumn, winter had come and gone. The pastures, the parks, the fields and the forests lay deserted, for people feared the giant devil worm, and cruel toll he took from town and village. No hope there seemed but that in time the smiling land should turn into the silent wilderness.

"At last the king, overwhelmed by the plight of his lieges, set out, clothed in chain armour,† mounted on his war-horse as of yore, his sword belted to his side, his dagger strapped to his arm. Alone he rode to conquer or to die that he might save his land and people from the

---

* This is a liberal translation into European imagery.

† Chain armour, dating from the times of the Crusades and the Saracens, is still used in the Sudan.

demon scourge. At noon he rode; at night he lay dead on the plain.

<small>He found, and fought, and fell.</small> "The oldest prince, burning with revenge, set out the following morning. He found the dragon, fought and fell. And mourning and wailing sounded through the land. The second prince arose; he fought and fell. The third, the fourth, the fifth, the sixth, the last, all dared and died.

"In hut and palace there was death-like silence. The overwhelming sorrow made men dumb, and women's tears had dried in mute despair.

"At midnight, on the ninth day, the yellow-grayish coils of the terrible beast, shimmering in phosphorescent light, glided towards the lonely homes of the widowed daughters of the fallen king. The bat-like wings raised the horrible body, the protruding flaming eyes appeared over the walls of the fort, which had been the home of the oldest prince, the long neck stretched itself, and the narrow head pushed through the door of the nursery of the new-born princeling. Two jets of fire exuded from the nostrils, and illuminated with their ghastly glare the little chamber. The cruel fangs closed over the sleeping infant. A shriek of pain from the fatherless, husbandless, childless widow and the tragedy was over.

"But the dragon did not kill the child. He carried it away back to its mountain den, and in a little cave he hid it. A second time he went, and the second child was lodged within a second cave. Thus on till all the seven children had been taken. Then, satiated with its evil deeds, the dragon lay himself, the devil Cerberus, between the seven infants in their mountain caves and seven mourning mothers in their lonely homes.

"See, white man, up yonder, the seven princesses in their seven castles, the seven princes in their seven caves, and in between the dragon's outstretched body."

The Ursa Major, Ursa Minor and the Dragon.

Innumerable tales the starry firmament provides for the dusky son of the dark Continent. Many a night have I lain by the camp-fire and listened to the oft brilliantly-told astronomical stories. But enough for to-night.

Astronomical Stories.

The fires are burning low.

The horses and oxen are munching behind the tent, the clammy night-fog rises from the brook.

It is time to rest. Good-night!

From Northern Nigeria to the Nile

From the Benué to Bor

> We stand in the midst of the thing Thou art doing;
> Give faith that our spirits may rise to Thy thought;
> Give courage with patience, though faint yet pursuing,
> Till following fully, we serve as we ought.

CHAPTER V

BLACK loomed the storm clouds in the east. Like the mighty billows of an ocean the tornado comes rolling down the valley of the Benué.

A small army of snow-flaked clouds, resembling a flock of sea-gulls before the hurricane, are the vanguard of the slatey, steel-coloured tumuli that turn blacker every moment. The hills, the river banks, the trees and bushes are blotted out, and a solid bank of inky black hides the horizon.

Before us lies not a pocketful of wind, but a whole world of wind.

"Hold on!"—the slim, top-heavy barge has bumped into the brown bank, the south bank of the river. "Hold on!—don't let her drift!"

Two white men scramble out of her, one with an anchor, the other with a line to make the barge fast just behind a corner of the land, caused by the bend of the river, round which the swirling deep water rushes in a rapid current. The anchor chain is wound round some bushes and a small tree, and the anchor itself buried into the ground. The waterproof side-curtains of the boat are let down, and securely tied, and

A Tornado.

wondering what is going to happen we wait for the storm.

You can see it coming, a ripple on the water, and a thick haze just above. Two or three sharp whistling blasts, and we are wrapped in the blanket of the whirl-wind which strives with all its might to lay low whatever is raised above earth's surface.

"Hold on, men! hold on! or we shall be blown away from the bank, and once we are away from that we are done for!" Intense suspense! Five minutes pass. There is a moment's lull, and then the rain commences. The worst is over. The velocity of the wind is still very great, the rain drops are driven almost horizontally, and sting into one's arms and face like pins and needles; but the critical moment has passed, and we can easily outlast the strong, steady current of air that sweeps down westward.

Shipwrecked.

Not a few canoes, barges and boats have been turned over by the tornadoes in the beginning of the rainy season. A little while ago three Government men were going up river in a steel boat, with all their belongings, for a year's sojourn in Northern Nigeria; food, clothing, pots and pans, rifles and ammunition, tents and saddles, and all the paraphernalia needed for life in the woods. When a tornado blew up they tried to get to the bank of the river, but the time was too short, and in the middle of the stream the boat was blown over and sank, and all their belongings were buried at the bottom of the Benué, or started swimming down stream. The shipwreck took place some distance away from the shore; the men had to divest themselves of some of their clothing to reach it, and when they got there they found themselves in an uninhabited part of the country. They made themselves turbans of grass to protect their heads against the fierce rays of the mid-day sun. All day they waited for some one to come along on the river. But no one came. They spent the night in a sad plight. They had no matches, and could not light a fire, and the night was cold. In addition to it all, it started raining, and the dawn found them with chattering teeth, an attack of malaria, and no brighter prospects than they had had on the previous day. Fortunately, a steamer came and picked up the castaways.

I was on my way up the Benué River when the previously mentioned tornado incident occurred; having begun my trans-African journey in earnest. Mr. Hosking, from South Africa, accompanied me. We were going in the boat as far as the river would float her, and then Mr. Hosking was to take her back to the Mission Stations of the Sudan United Mission.

The river was alive with water fowl; ducks and geese, teal and snipe, cranes and crown-birds, pelicans and the burun-tunki, a bird that looks as strange as its name, a tall black and white bird, much taller than a stork, with a heavy beak. It walks in a most solemn, stately style, having no communion with any other birds, in lonely grandeur on the sandbanks or the fish-abounding shallows. American missionaries named these

"Close Communion Baptists."

birds in my hearing, "Close Communion Baptists!"

Hardly ever have I tasted as delicious ducks, teal and geese as on the Upper Benuê. Two or three antelopes also found their way into our larder, and pleased our boatmen not a little.

The lazy, languid progress on the water was an excellent tonic, and reminds one of the sleepy progress of a drifting Nile dahabiah. The frequent calls from other boats as we passed them, "*Sanu, sanu!*" (Slowly, slowly), sounded like irony. "*Sanu, sanu*" is the Hausa salutation, and illustrates the mode of progress of Central Africa, which is very *sanu, sanu*.

"Sanu! Sanu!"

It is remarkable how different nationalities are characterised by their salutations. An Englishman meeting another says "How do you do?" The busy business man, the glorified "shopkeeper" of Napoleon, the Britisher, is always wanting to do something, and some, including our cousins in the New World, somebody! The Germans meeting on the road call out "Wie geht es Ihnen?" (How does it walk you? How do you progress?) The Germans are progressing at such a rate, let us see to it—in friendly rivalry—that they do not progress past us. The French, the fathers of fashion, salute each other most solemnly, "Comment vous portez-vous?" (How do you carry yourself? How do you dress yourself?) The Latin races, Italian, Spanish, Portuguese, whose progress has been but little during the last five hundred years, bid welcome to each other with the sentence

"Comme sta?" (How do you stand?) They stood, and they stand still. In the Scriptural phrase, "What shall we eat, what shall we drink, and wherewithal shall we be clothed," the Chinaman, a member of the greatest heathen nation, concerned about his food and drink and clothing, asks, "Have you had your rice?" The early Christians greeted each other with the central fact of their faith, the foundation of their hope, "The Lord is risen!" and the answer to it, "The Lord is risen indeed!"

The Arab, whose religion leads to war, will never salute a Christian with "Salaam-aleikum," (Peace be with you.) And the Hausa, as we saw in the beginning, bids his friend upon the road go "*Sanu, sanu!*" (Slowly! slowly!)

A district I had especially in mind, and where I desired to investigate the possibilities for successful Mission work, was the Djen district. On a Saturday afternoon we came to the large sandbank which has been formed by the river in front of the town of Djen. One calls Djen a town, but it really is a number of hamlets inhabited by some savage-looking pagans. Mr. Hosking and I thought a good means of introduction would be to go out to secure some meat for the villagers. We were told that large numbers of antelopes lived in a plain a mile away from the place where we had pitched the tent. Several of the natives came along with us, but fortune did not favour me that night, and in spite of firing at several, I failed to bring home a solitary buck.

Djen, the hamlet town.

Mr. Hosking was more fortunate, and bagged two.

Weary and hungry we returned to the tent, and left the meat to be divided by the villagers. Night had fallen. A large camp fire had been lit, and we were resting in the cool of the evening, when the people brought the game. With much vociferation and with angry shouts, they appealed to me to adjudge quarrels that had arisen in their appropriation of the venison. They began gesticulating with their spears and knives; some fifty or a hundred savage-looking men. And as none of our party knew their language, and the one or two of them who knew a certain amount of Hausa had gone to their huts, it was difficult to know what to do with them. It looked as if within a short time bloodshed would ensue, and they would fight and kill each other. My head boy, Dan, who stood behind me, whispered that matters were beginning to look ugly.

"Bring out my signalling pistol, Dan."

The rocket. Quickly the little weapon, containing a green rocket, was placed into my hands. A moment more I waited. What would happen? As the quarrel waxed fast and furious, I fired. Upon the loud detonation there followed sudden silence, and as the green fire-ball spun upwards, far beyond the height of the tallest trees, up and up towards the stars, the weird, angry faces of the mob took on a look of awe. Great eyeballs stared out of astonished faces, wide open mouths that had just ejaculated vituperative screams forgot to close. One after another crept away, and peace, perfect peace, reigned through the silent night.

*   *   *   *

"Say, Hosking! this looks a splendid place for a successful Mission Station!"

For two miles we had passed nothing but houses, village upon village on the south bank of the Benué, and still there were more villages ahead as far as the eye could reach.

We had come to the M'bula country. The Djen district lay behind us; where once we had thought of establishing the Lucy Memorial Freed Slaves' Home. But the low-lying land, which was evidently one vast swamp in the rainy season, marked it as an unhealthy, fever place, and not suitable for permanent occupation by a white man, or a Home for our freed slaves' children. We had passed the mouth of the Gongola river that comes down from the Bauchi hill country, and in the rainy season carries great volumes of water. We had visited Numan, lying opposite the mouth of the Gongola, with its Government post, its Hausa traders, and its many fishermen. And now we had come to the most densely populated part of the Benué valley. North of M'bula several hills showed on the horizon, inhabited by the Tangele pagans; wild, obstreperous people that are still giving trouble to the Government. And while M'bula itself, a district containing some fifteen villages, has a good deal of swampy ground between the different centres of population, on the opposite side of the river the hills come within half a mile of the edge of the water, and the

M'bula and the Tangele pagans.

ground is dry enough to augur absence of fever.

Both Mr. Hosking and I were much impressed with the suitability of this site to form a basis for the South African branch of the Sudan United Mission. And when later the Resident of the Yola Province expressed his sincere approval of our choice, saying that from the Government standpoint he would be glad to have one or two white men living amongst the M'bula people, the indications for permanent satisfactory work among the afore-named tribe were most apparent. To-day the Mission has its station in that district, and Messrs. Hosking, Botha, and Zimmermann have made a promising beginning.

The object of the trans-African journey. To carry the reader from place to place on this prolonged and interesting expedition is impossible in this book. But a few outstanding incidents and scenes may not be without value to the central argument of it. To begin with, it is well to state that this journey was not an evangelistic tour. And while on Sundays there were regular services with the men, and quiet chats along the way and in the evenings, no attempt was made to reach the pagans through interpreters with the Gospel. And the following were the reasons:

(*a*) An interpreter's knowledge of the languages in which I could make myself understood was usually confined to one or two hundred words.

(*b*) The interpreter, too, would have but a faint conception of the religion of the white man, in spite of quiet talks and the Sunday services.

(c) The interpreter's knowledge of the pagan language was usually found less than his knowledge of Hausa or Arabic, English or French.

Thus to preach through an interpreter as mouth-piece would have been utter folly, and might have given the very opposite idea of what the writer meant to say. The journey was simply a tour of investigation to visit the pagan tribes, collect a few vocabularies in the most important languages, secure information as to the advance of Mohammedanism, and gather knowledge and facts geographical, ethnological, botanical, and zoological.

The zoological and botanical knowledge of these regions determine the food supplies which future missionaries may have to take; meteorological knowledge and geographical knowledge permit calculation as to the comparative healthiness of various districts, while philological knowledge is, of course, the basis of all educational and evangelistic work.

Before sending missionaries to various parts of the Sudan, the conditions of life there, distribution of population, accessibility or otherwise of these regions, had to be determined; and it was this that the expedition essayed to do, and to a certain extent achieved.

The accomplishment of this involved difficulties and dangers not a few. After a farewell dinner in Yola, the last British post in Northern Nigeria, the Resident of that Province, in bidding

Farewell Dinner.

God-speed to me, expressed his good wishes in the following terms:—

Good wishes for the road.

"Dr. Kumm, I wish you luck, and every success. I hope the cannibals won't eat you, and the wild beasts won't trouble you, and the fanatics won't kill you. I hope you won't die of fever or sleeping-sickness, or be drowned in the swamps and rivers, or be starved in the uninhabited bush. I wish you every luck."

* * * *

"Lululu!—Lululu!—lulululululu!" (Welcome, welcome, welcome!) the shrill falsetto voices of the women screamed out their *bien venue*.

"Lululu! Lululu!"

"Lululu—Ya—Sayid!" (Welcome, oh lord!) The Central African "lululu" is a savage modernisation of the old Hebrew "hallelujah,— Praise to Jah, praise to Jehovah!"

From every native compound, from all the little lanes, from every rock and vantage ground, the high notes assailed us as we rode up towards the town of Mandjafa, after having crossed the Shari River—a wild welcome—to the French Bagirmi Central Sudan regions. The chief, with his councillors, had come down to the river sandbanks to meet us; gorgeously-bedecked very fat horses, war-drums and war-horns, the clash of swords and spears, a confused medley of sights and sounds greeted us. The chief's interpreter pressed up to my horse.

"Marhaba - Ya - Nassara." "Welcome, oh Christian! The king bids you welcome. Your messengers arrived and told us of your coming, and we are glad that you are here."

After another outburst of luluing, the chief puts the spurs into his horse, that rears up on its hind legs—to be able to make a horse walk on its hind legs while mounted on it seems to be the pride of all savage chiefs—threw it round on its haunches, and careered up the steep clay bank towards his town. More steady and stately, the white man followed, with carriers and village folk pressing behind him in great confusion.

" Where is my camping-ground, chief ? "

To my amusement, arrangements for our arrival had been altogether forgotten over the luluing and the shouting of welcome, and it took half an hour before a suitable compound was prepared. Hedges of native grass matting form labyrinths of the native courtyards, and turn them into intricate habitations like rabbit warrens. One of the largest of these compounds, on the edge of the river bank, was cleared out, the hedges swept away, and, after awhile, an open space of some fifty yards by fifty obtained. In the centre of it a sun shelter was erected, a tent pitched, and about a dozen huts that lay around this compound were occupied by the carriers and boys.

Preparing a Camp.

The march through German Adamawa had, against all expectations, been most unexciting. Neither the savage Lam Pagans, nor the fanatical Marua people, nor, for the matter of that, the Musgun warriors, had given any trouble. On the contrary, they had opened their homes to us, supplied food, and cheered the caravan on its road. And now a similar welcome, prepared for the caravan, on its entering the Shari-Chad Protectorate, promised well for the success of the attempted traverse of the Sudan.

How many fights?

The Chief Constable of Glasgow asked me after one of my addresses in that city: " Dr. Kumm, how many times did you fight to get through the savage tribes of the Sudan ? "

" I did not fight."

" Surely you must have fought. See, Stanley, coming down the Congo, fought twenty-eight pitched battles. Boyd Alexander fought ; Hans Vischer fought. Surely you must have fought. How many people did you kill while crossing ? "

" I neither fought nor killed."

" But, surely, you must have found inimical savages! What did they do when you came to their villages ? "

" They ran until we made friends."

There was no need for me to fight. Let me reiterate what I have said before in other publications.

What we call into a wood we get back as the echo.

What we call into a wood we get back as the echo. The Golden rule holds good in Africa as well as at home, " Do unto others as you would have them do to you." I take no special credit to myself. The combination of circumstances was an unusual one. The two or three points at which I had to deal with Moslem fanatics were the most dangerous. Happily, these religious antagonists happened to be in a friendly mood.

And luck, or, as I would like to call it,

NORTHERN NIGERIA TO THE NILE

Providence, permitted the success, prepared the way, provided for the needs, gave perseverance and persistence in hope till the end was attained. In the German Kameruns I was warned by the Government representative not to attempt the traverse of the country of the Lam Pagans, and to keep out of Marua, where a German officer had been killed less than a twelve-month before. In the Shari Valley the French officials and traders were afraid that in Sinussi's country I would find an end to my expedition. And when, on my arrival in the Eastern Sudan, the Sudd region blocked my way after the severe nervous and physical strain that I had undergone in traversing certain uninhabited districts of the Central Sudan, and threatened a final breakdown, a certain reserve stock of patience and will power from the El-Shaddaic (All-Sufficient) source was just sufficient.

* * * *

With a ceaseless swish and clatter the stern wheels drive the boat through the muddy waters of the Bahr-el-Jebel (the mountain river), usually known as the White Nile. We pass along between narrow banks of everlasting papyrus rolling, rising, and falling as the waves caused by our boat carry their slanting shapes against the mass of floating vegetation. From the top of the mast one vast sea of broom-headed reeds, reeds, nothing but reeds, stretches from east to west, from north to south as far as the eye can reach. Open lagoons, rifts and rivers, appear here and there; *The Great Sudd.*

yonder, to the right, some four miles away, a solitary bush grows on some lonely island.

Great flocks of birds circle round our boat with scream and screech, while ugly moss-backed ancient dwellers of the deep, gray horn-sheathed crocodiles, lie sunning themselves on the rare mud banks.

In certain places the floating vegetation is so thick that herds of elephants can march over the heaving mass without sinking through it. In other places again small floating islands, carried round and round by the current, come sailing down the stream or lie marooned in some back-water or corner of a lake.

The bellowing of a herd of hippos is carried towards us through the still air of the late afternoon.

Unwieldy tree-trunks, misshaped dug-outs, carrying two or three giant-limbed Dinkas, creep out behind us from some side-lane, and speed up the river whence we came. The desperate monotony of the Sudd becomes enlivened nightly by mosquitoes, which, as a permanent plague, make life to any white man there a burden. Just on the south edge of this great Sudd region two devoted C.M.S. missionaries at Bor Station have begun successfully to instil into the Dinkas the rudiments of our faith in Christ.

Giants and their pigmy neighbours.

The people living in this greatest swamp on earth, where neither tree nor rock nor mountain ever gives the slightest shade, and the brilliant sun of the tropics blazes down from morning till night relentlessly on the open watery plain, have grown up until they have become the giants of the human race. The shadeless sun and the swampy ground have developed limbs of abnormal length, while but a few hundred miles to the south-east the eternal shadows of the Ituri forests have stunted the growth of their inhabitants, and produced a race of dwarfs, the pigmies. Thus, in the Sudan regions, " *les extrémes se touches.*"

When, on the first night in the Khartum Hotel on my arrival from the bush, I woke up before the morning unaccustomed to the walls and the roof of a room which kept out fresh air, and felt oppressive, and as the many instances in which death seemed much more probable than life passed unwittingly in review, I found myself burst out into a jarring laugh. It seemed so incredible that I should have come across the Continent, without losing any of my carriers, in better health than when I started. With a sudden jerk the laugh broke; I knelt beside my bed and thanked God for the prayers of my fellow-workers at home who had laboured on my behalf, and for a life brought back out of the shadows of death to be used henceforth in more devoted service.

Khartum at last.

Hunting in Africa : Slaves and Animals

(Freed Slaves' Home)

"*Campiere oft zur Winterszeit,*
Bei Sturm und Wetternacht,
Hab' ueberreift und euberschneit,
Den Stein zum Bett gemacht.

Ein Tannreis schmueckt stat Blumenzier,
Den schweissbedeckten Hut,
Und dennoch schlug die Liebe mir
In's wilde Jaegerblut."

CHAPTER VI

SQUEAL!!!—squeal!—squeal!
And I got him, a baby boar who had wandered away from his mother in the old home forests near the "Teufelsloch."

The wee, pretty little beastie! How he kicked and screamed, his striped body quivering with excitement.

I was the proud possessor of a young wild-pig.
Carefully I picked him up and held him in my arms, while squeal after squeal resounded through the forest, the "Help!—help!—help!" of the little fellow. And help came sooner than I wanted or had expected. For with a mighty rush the old sow came blundering through the undergrowth, down the hillside.

The captive.

There is no playing with savage sows, and counting discretion the better part of valour, I scrambled up into the low-hanging branches of an old fir-tree, still holding on to my kicking captive. I just managed to get up the tree when the mother arrived, and with a furious grunt, halted a yard or two beneath me, rolled her savage little eyes, gave another grunt, and tried to climb the tree; which, of course, was no good.

After two or three vain attempts to get at me, she gave it up, and marched snorting round the foot of my shelter, stepped back five yards, and looked at me, with eyes that said, "You come down, and I will pay you out for making my baby squeal!"

Siege to the captor.
For some five minutes the boy and the mother-pig watched each other; the boy, who was only twelve years old, would hardly have been a proper boy, had he not appropriated the pig when the opportunity offered. But what to do now that he had got it—that was where the rub came in. Whose patience would last the longest, the boy's in the tree, or the sow's at the foot? It was five o'clock in the afternoon of a winter's day, and the sun would be down in twenty minutes.

Most reluctantly the boy agreed to release his little brown beauty that kept on singing, singing lustily. Carefully he lowered it till it fell on its four stumpy little legs. With a joyful snort mother and child met, and without looking round, trotted back to the shadows of the thicket.

What is it that makes a hunter, or that creates the instinct—the longing for the chase? Surely it is not the lust of blood or the desire to kill with the true trapper, the fast friend of the forest.

True hunting instincts.
There are two kinds of hunting, one that is justified, and the other that is not. The first is the sportsmanlike pitting of the brawn and brain of the hunter against the brawn and brain of the hunted.

With lion and elephant, leopard and boar, the fight is quite fair. There are men-eating lions, and there are lion-eating men. There are men-killing elephants, and there are elephant-killing men.

Hunting with primitive weapons of large game is good exercise. And to shoot for the pot needs no justification.

As to the second kind of hunting, that is an entirely different affair, and neither manly nor sportsmanlike. To go with a modern weapon, shooting cordite, and massacre giraffes or antelopes, male and female and young alike; to shoot for the sake of shooting and kill for the sake of killing, is not Christian, is not human. To turn a Maxim gun on to a herd of hartebeest is not sportsmanlike.

For two boys or two young men to measure their strength in wrestling is a play and a pastime to be encouraged; but for a strong man to beat the weak, for intelligent men armed with heavy weapons of offence and defence to enslave the ignorant is unmanly and un-Christian.

The life in the wilds reveals the primeval tendencies for good or evil.

Let us now look at a few instances of what I mean.

Hungry eyes looked at me. Skin and bone limbs seemed more ready for the grave than for a two thousand mile march.

"*Min fadlak*" (Of your kindness), "we beg of you to let us come with you to the Nile. We are on our way to Mecca. We were left behind two months ago because we were too weak to continue, but now we are strong." *Moslem pilgrims.*

"Strong, indeed! What have you been living on these two months?"

"Roots and leaves."

"You look like it. How far do you think you could march?"

"*Allah jaaref*" (God knows!)

"Yes, indeed God knows, for I know not."

The two or three hungry-looking people desire to swell my Hausa-Mecca-pilgrim-caravan that has already attained considerable dimensions. Hesitatingly I give my permission for these poor devoted Moslems to follow me. Shall I turn them away because Christians never gave them a chance to know the true Christ? Surely I will not.

Next morning the caravan moves on. Tracks of elephants, buffaloes, giraffes, criss-cross the bush path. One of the French Guards that accompanied me states that in less than three hours we shall be on the banks of the Ba River, and that there are hippos in that river. Beyond the river lie several days of uninhabited bush, the border regions of the Sinussi country of Dar-Kuti.

Dan sidles up to me.

"Please sir, the people want meat."

"Yes, Dan. Where are we to get it?"

"Please, sir, there are hippos in the Ba."

"All right, we'll see."

Hippos for food. When a line of tall trees that marked the bank of the stream appeared, I left my caravan behind, and cantering ahead dismounted. Carefully I stalked through the long elephant grass towards the edge of the river bank, which was some twelve or fifteen feet above a deep muddy pool. Lumps of refuse floating on the water told the tale, and silently I lay low, a .405 Winchester in my hand, loaded with hard-nosed bullets. The water was without a ripple, still as a millpond.

By the muddy pool.

Look! Hardly thirty yards away, without the least sound, two short pokey ears, two bulging eyes, and a massive square-jawed head appeared. The nostrils opened, and with a disconcerting snort, the giant of the deep was about to sink again when the missile from my rifle sped on its way, and lodged true through inch-thick skin, through half a foot of cartilage and bone, in the brain-pan of the beast. As if struck with lightning the mighty animal reared itself out of the water, turned over on its back, gave two or three violent kicks with the stumpy legs, and sank. As one body disappeared, another head, belonging to the father of the herd, came to the surface. He, too, received his ball. But whether the age of the animal, and consequently the thickness of the bone was greater than that of the former beast, and therefore had a greater power of resistance,—whatever it was, instead of sinking, with several frantic jerks the hippo struggled to the other shore, got into the shallows, and rose. But another steel cone drilled its way through its head, and, without a sound or single movement, it subsided.

The joy of the people, the rejoicing of the Mecca pilgrims when they came up and we forded the river some two hundred yards away from the hippo pool, the broad smiles on the emaciated, half-starved faces of old and young, were the justification for supplying food to the hungry ones. They lifted their thin fists and shook them at me, attempting to convey their faith in my protecting and providing strength. How simple, childlike, light-lived these people are.

Like a village fair.

The Ba River camp within an hour after our arrival looked like a village fair. There was music, there was feasting, there was sunshine, there was life. The women went to the water and washed their clothes in honour of the occasion; the men set to work with their knives, their spears and tomahawks, to divide the bodies of the two great water beasts which had been hauled up to the bank. And with two antelopes, shot earlier in the morning, there was now meat enough to last us to Ndele.

True trappers and nidering cowards.

The game of the wilderness is given by God as food for men, but to massacre animal life in order that one may indulge in the pleasure of killing has no justification. The vast herds of bison once inhabiting the United States were slaughtered by unscrupulous butchers, who were neither true trappers nor honourable huntsmen. The unnumbered herds of antelopes that once lived in South Africa have been decimated and redecimated until, with the exception of a few small private flocks, all have been slain.

Into all European Colonies in Africa satisfactory game laws have now, one is thankful to say, been introduced.

If men killed men in warfare they were justified by our forefathers, but to slay women and children was the work of *nidering* cowards. To slaughter the females and the young of game is not in harmony with the spirit of true Saxon hunters. Giraffes and rhinos, hippos and zebras have been exterminated in, or driven out of, many parts of Africa, and the only animal that seems to be able to resist the onslaught and depredations of men is the elephant, who, while the least prolific and the easiest to trace, is yet most difficult to find. It is almost omnipresent south of the Sahara. That is to say, there are elephants in Cape Colony, elephants in East Africa, elephants in West Africa, there are elephants all through the Sudan, there are elephants in the Congo valley, in British Central Africa, on the Zambesi, there are elephants in Uganda, in Abyssinia, and in the Galla country.

In spite of their great size they are hard to see, and in spite of their apparent spoor they are not easy to come up with, as they usually indulge in a morning's constitutional of some twenty or thirty miles. Following the spoor of elephants means days of tracking, and one has wondered sometimes whether these great pachyderms can be walking right across the Continent, and appear now in East Africa, now in West Africa.

<small>Across a continent for a constitu= tional.</small>

They seem to be continually on the move, with the exception of a couple of hours' rest in the middle of the day. They are stout-hearted, clever animals. One of them, shot by me, had a double heart. The herd out of which this one was secured was a very remarkable one, as amongst their number there was another heavy beast with four tusks.

Besides elephants and antelopes, there is another game that is hunted in Africa. Its name is slave. Permit a few incidents as they were reported by missionaries of the Sudan United Mission.

(From Mr. T. L. Maxwell, Superintendent of the S.U.M. in Northern Nigeria, and others).

"To-day, a German, a Mr. Habisch, came to see me with a little quadroon boy called Ibrahim, whom he asked me to take and educate, which, of course, I agreed to do. So, in a day or two, Ibrahim is to be in my hands. Mr. H.'s conversation proved most interesting. He has been out eight years without being home, and has travelled a good deal. One or two things he told me will interest you.

"He spoke of the Basel Mission work at Bamum, how friendly the king there is, how he asked for the missionary or missionaries from Bali (a station some distance away), and how he himself provided the carriers for them, built their houses, pulled down the mosque, built the church, attends it every Sunday with hundreds of his people, and has instituted a system of compulsory education in his town. Wonderful and pleasant to hear of. Doesn't it remind you of the text, 'The queen of the south . . . . came from the uttermost parts of the earth.' To think of it forcibly suggests Uganda. Now, may God send us many a Uganda here in the west for His Son's glory.

"Another thing he told me is sad—very, very sad. Look up Ngaumdere, in Adamawa; it is about the centre of it, a little to the north. From there towards the French Congo runs a road—the Hanyan Yaki 'War Road'—which Mr. H. tells me is marked by human bones. This is the road along which the Fullahs from Ngaumdere brought the slaves from their raids into the Laka territory, and the bones *even now* are the sign-posts of the road, though, since 1902, the trade has been stopped.

"As I am writing, my little boy Rabo, who is a Laka, has come in. He is only a child of about twelve years old, but he remembers the time when *he* was brought from Laka to Ngaumdere. He tells me how he has seen slaves, who refused to go on, clubbed to death and cut down with swords. He has seen his brother brained with a stone, and his father shot and killed with a poisoned arrow in the fight, after which he himself was captured. And he is only a *little* boy.

"Sit down quietly, and think what it means. Add up the columns, total up the misery that it means that this *one* lad should be here to-day, and then go quietly and thank the merciful Father Who brought *your* fathers the Bible, and the Saviour, Whose freedom has made *you* free. Thank Him not in vain words dropped from careless lips, but in hot-hearted love language that shall echo through every moment of your life. Thank God! oh! a thousand times thank God, for the light that has lightened *our* land. Thank God that *He* does not forget, and *He* has

Human Sign-posts.

Remembered by a boy of twelve.

remembered Africa, and the slave is even now being freed.

> 'A cry of tears goes up from blackened homesteads,
>   A cry of blood goes up from reeking earth,
> Tears and blood have a cry that reaches heaven
>   Through all its hallelujah swells of mirth;
>   God hears their voice, and, though He tarry, yet He doth not forget.'

"To-day slave dealing is punishable with death in German Adamawa. Men have been arrested on the road, and, confessing their guilt, have been summarily shot. It is punishable with penal servitude in British territory. The other day the Resident here at Ibi, referring to a gang of convicts close at hand, told me that most of them were imprisoned for slave dealing."

Another incident.

"Recently there was brought into our compound at Wukari a middle-aged woman, careworn, bruised, lash-marked, and nearly exhausted. From her home in Adamawa she had been stolen from her husband and family, and sold into slavery. Twice she had changed masters. She had been brought to this town by the Fulani. When she spoke to her master concerning her desire to be free, he immediately bound her and beat her severely, as the marks upon her back clearly showed. Fearing that she would run away, he decided to sell her. With her hands tightly bound to her left shoulder he set off with her to a suitable market. During the night she made good her escape. Two nights, without food or shelter, she had hidden away in the 'bush.'

Bound and Beaten.

Here she was found by two native traders, who unbound her, and brought her to us. It was our pleasure to turn her over to the Resident, who set her free. Her master, fearing punishment, disappeared.

"A small boy, a brother of the liberated woman, was also under the same master. For him she earnestly pleaded. He was in charge of the cattle. Early in the morning, without food, he was sent out with the cattle. He watched over them during the day, and brought them home at night. In the evening he sat down to a scanty meal of gruel. Numerous other duties were assigned him. When he hesitated he was cruelly beaten, or burned with coals of fire. Hungry, bruised, and scarred, he was found by a labourer, and his case was put in the hands of the Resident.

"On the Benué the traffic in slaves is still carried on quite extensively. In such centres as Yola and Ibi there is barter in human beings almost daily. The Government is doing its best to break it up, but much of it is done so secretly that the guilty parties are not easily discovered. Not long since a certain Resident saw a canoe filled with women and children passing his town. He ordered the boat to be stopped, and an investigation made. The man in charge of the canoe insisted that the women were his wives, and the boys and girls his children. Upon further examination it was found that none of them could understand the language of the canoe-man. They were all slaves that had been taken

Children who could not speak their father's language.

from some region in the East, and were being taken to a down-river market. They were freed, and their master dealt with according to law.

"On another occasion a Kakanda canoe was searched, and some children were found lying in the bottom of it, covered over by large grass mats. This is quite a common way of concealing them during a halt at a town or when they are passing the 'white man's' boat.

An Escape to the White Man.

"A little boy had been brought by a slave-trader from Adamawa, his wily master having previously carefully marked this boy and two girl slaves with his own tribal marks, so that he might pass them off as his own children. They travelled down river (the Benué) till they came to Rumasha, *and here his master managed to sell the boy on the quiet.*

"He did not look starved, so we asked him if his old master had been good to him. We gathered that while in his own country he had not treated him well, but since arriving in Northern Nigeria he had been much more gentle in his dealings—which speaks well for the firmness of our Government in putting an end to the old-time cruelties. The laddie told us he had been put into an inner room by his new master, but somehow had managed to break through, and make a dash for liberty. While in Rumasha he had heard of the white man being in the vicinity, and had evidently learned that the said white man was putting an end to slave dealing.

"When asked if we took him up to Rumasha could he point out the man who bought him, he promptly replied, 'Yes, he could, if the man did not run away when he saw white man coming.' A pretty smart reply, seeing that it was more than likely that the gentleman would have adopted that course, as there is now a heavy punishment for buying or selling a slave. He was also asked how he proposed to get his food if we set him free, and again the reply was apt, and yet pathetic, '*Only you can tell that.*' We told him he was free, and no one could take him back to slavery.

Only you can tell that.

"After he was received, we clothed him in a suit of garments from home. It was quite nice to hear of the head man of the brickmakers, Zegi, a fine old chap who wants to be taught about Jesus, fussing round the laddie, and seeing that his garments fitted. The boy was handed over to Tom's care. One could see Tom's heart was in his mouth as he remembered his own liberation by Sir William Wallace at Lokoja."

The Sudan United Mission has been asked by the Government to take charge of the liberated slave children in Northern Nigeria and has agreed to do so. The Lucy Memorial Freed Slaves' Home, built in memory of my late wife, has now been in existence for eighteen months, and is doing good work. The following few pages contain reports and information about this Home.

The Lucy Memorial Freed Slaves' Home.

"The site of the 'Lucy Memorial' Freed Slaves' Home is an elevated ridge on the north side of the river Benué, running parallel with the river. It lies about one-third of a mile from the river bank, from which it rises by a gradual

Situation and Climate.

slope until it attains an elevation of about 100 feet above the high-water mark. The view is a very beautiful one, not easily surpassed in Nigeria. In front and below flow the broad, placid waters of the Benué, more than a mile in width, beyond lies the river valley covered with dense tropical forest, and beyond the forest rise the blue-green hills of the Bassa country in serried ranks, attaining an elevation of some 700-800 feet.

"The soil is porous and gravelly, and absorbs rainfall so readily that it never gets sodden, even during the frequent rains of the wet season. This fact should contribute much towards freedom from malaria, and general good health. There is an abundance of good timber around, which will be a valuable feature when our boys begin to learn woodworking.

"The total number of children we have taken over from the Government is 182. Of these only fifty-two are boys, of the following ages:—

Kura.

"Three of 14, three of 11 to 12, fourteen of 8 to 10, and thirty-two under 8. One is semi-insane, and almost blind. He is from a cannibal tribe, has cannibal proclivities, and needs to be watched, as he is frequently disposed to take a bite out of the anatomy of his little brethren. He goes by the name of Kura, which is the Hausa name for hyena, and in this case there is 'something in a name.'

"Of the girls and women there are 130, as follows:—

"Four women of 20 years and over, seven girls of 14 to 18 years, thirty-one girls of 10 to 14, twenty-eight of 8 to 10, thirty-two of 7, twenty-eight under 7 years.

"The children are well-disciplined and obedient, and seem bright and happy. They are from many different tribes, and speak many languages. Little toddlers, some of them, who have been sold almost from their mother's breast, in times of want and famine. Others doubtless have been taken in slave raids, far in the interior, where European Government has not yet put a stop to that curse of Africa.

"A large number of these children came down from the Province of Bornu, some two years ago. They were in the charge of English officers, and at a certain stage of the journey it was noticed that three of them were missing from the number. A halt was made, and a search for the missing ones instituted. After considerable delay (about two days, I believe), they were found; that is, two of them, and what remained of the third, for when the officers came upon them, they found the two in the act of roasting and eating the third one. Whether these two had deliberately killed their companion, or whether he had come to his death some other way—and they only decided to eat him after he was dead—is not known. One of the two survivors was our Kura previously alluded to. He was not at that time affected by the eye disease which has since rendered him almost blind." *Child Cannibals.*

How near akin to beasts of prey! Yet even in the lowest of the low, as they are members of the human family, there is the spark divine, the *The Spark Divine.*

feeling after God, the possibility of the higher life.

"A few small girls are standing around me, wrapped in blankets. They seem to feel the cold of the mornings very much. One of them—Jibi—has been ill a long time in hospital, and on Tuesday it was thought she would have to be re-admitted. Jibi much prefers being out of hospital, though she is very fond of 'ligita' (doctor). In the afternoon, Jibi begged most piteously that he would allow her to get up, and offered him a headless doll, minus clothing. However, he refused the bribe. She thereupon tried another doll, headless, but *with* clothing. That having no effect either, she promptly borrowed a resplendent doll from the girl in the next bed, and offered that to try and melt his hard heart. Fortunately, Jibi was able to be up next day, and is now quite lively again.

"One small girl passed along a short time ago, carrying something very tenderly in her arms. I called her, and asked her where she was going. She showed me a very rueful countenance, and pointed to a big crack in her dolly's head, saying, ' I am going to ask doctor for medicine for dolly!' Off she trotted, and returned a few minutes later, all smiles. Doctor had told her to put her doll to bed, and he would come over later to see it.

"The wee boys are most amusing specimens. One goes about solemnly with a big stick and a look of profound wisdom on his fat little face, and we call him 'Socrates.' Another mite says he is the king of Zunguru, and sings a most unintelligible medley, accompanied by a peculiar arm motion. The bigger boys work well, but the wee chaps are left pretty much free."

And now a report from the Home just to hand.

"About 9.30 a.m., when the work of the day was in full swing, a steamer whistle sounded near the Camp, and in a few minutes the large steamer 'Quorra' came in view, and turned into our beach. The Governor of the land, His Excellency Sir H. Hesketh Bell, had come to inspect the Home. What would be his impressions of the place, the children, the arrangements, the order, etc.? It was a beautiful bright morning; the sun was shining, the sky was blue, and the hills beyond the river stood out in clear relief. *A Governor's Inspection.*

"Here to the right is a group of our 'babies' at work, gathering gravel into small tins. These, when full, they place on their heads, and march off in single file to the path which they are filling with pebbles. Away to our left are a number of bigger girls 'weeding' in the farm, other girls at the back are busy washing clothes, others in the kitchen are preparing food; others, again, in the laundry room ironing, while down near the beach the boys are working on the farm.

"Such was the scene as it presented itself to the eyes of our visitors. Hospital work was just finished. Miss McNaught's Morning School was over, Miss Musgrave's time with the 'Hausa Malam' had come to an end, and we were ready to receive our guests. We found ourselves warmly shaken by the hand by His Excellency, and were soon engrossed in a quiet homely, friendly chat while our visitors were taking tea.

"H. E. evinced a keen interest in all that was going on around, asking many questions regarding the children, their capacity for learning, etc., and was quite interested seeing the 'little tots' at work!

"We called one of them, a bright little girl, 'Kelu,' who has been in hospital for a few days, but was out and at work to-day. She smiled broadly, and when touched, put out her tongue, evidently thinking it was a medical examination she was undergoing. Then we called 'Fatty.' Her name is indicative of herself. She came marching up as solemn as a judge, with never a smile on her face, rolling her black eyes from side to side and gazing now at one, now at another, as though she was wondering in her little mind what was going to happen. One of our visitors, taking a biscuit from a plate, offered it to her. She accepted it after a moment's hesitation, with a little curtsey and a half-whispered '*Na gode*' (I thank you).

Kelu and Fatty.

"Still another was brought, whose face showed so many cicatrices (tribal marks) that hardly a plain piece of skin remained.

"The Governor then expressed a desire to take a photograph of some of the little ones. About twenty-five were called up. They were placed together and then snapped by his Excellency. He seemed delighted with their bright faces and healthy looks, and said how very different they looked from the children up country.

"In the afternoon the children had a half-holiday in honour of the Governor's visit."

Why add words? Why a conclusion to this chapter? The facts depicted in it speak for themselves. Yet would the writer be at fault did he not draw, albeit in few words, a sum total.

The sum total.

(a) Slave-trading is being put down by the Christian Government representatives with a strong hand.

(b) Wild game in Africa is being protected against unscrupulous butchers.

(c) Should Central Africa be won for the Crescent faith, the teaching of the Koran, such as "It has not been granted unto any prophet, that he should possess slaves, until he has made a great slaughter of the infidels in the earth" (pages 375 and 133, Sales' Translation), will come into working, and newly-generated fanaticism result in the reintroduction of all the horrors of war and bloodshed, of rapine and slave raiding, and the half-healed sores of that Continent being torn open again.

Mohammedanism, with a Short History of Sinussiism

> Writ wide across the pages
>   Of continents outspread,
> The desert track of ages
>   Lies whitened with our dead;
> Through weary years of travel
>   We seek the Prophet's tomb,
> Nor find the Haj unravel
>   Life's mystery and gloom.

CHAPTER VII

BOOKS upon books have been written about Mohammedanism, the evolution of it, the operations of it, the fruits of it, that to generalise or repeat what has been said before would simply mean wasting one's energies. Still, there appears one aspect of Islam that has not yet been adequately worked out, and that is the influence, from the philosophical standpoint, which Mohammedanism has had and is having in Africa.

Mohammedanism has essayed to conquer the three Continents of the Old World. After running like wild-fire along the north coast of Africa it penetrated into Europe, and seriously set itself the task of ousting the faith in the Trinity from Europe. The bloody slaughter of Tours and Poitiers on the 10th of October, 732, in which the flower of the Norman and Saxon tribes under Charles Martel (the Hammer) barred the further advance of the Moorish hordes that had trekked through Spain and Portugal, through the South of Italy, and the South of France, driving the Latin races before them as spray before the autumn storm. But they broke their heads against the granite strength of the

Attempted Moslem Conquest of the world.

Franks, the Saxons, the Longbeards, the Alemans, the Germanic heart of Europe.

The Fall of Constantinople. Islam failed in its attempt from the south-west to conquer our northern Continent. For seven hundred years the black war-cloud hung over the Mediterranean between the Christian knights and the Paynim Moslems; but in 1453 the Crescent faith, having changed its objective from the south-west to the south-east, succeeded in ousting Christianity from the capital of Eastern Europe, Constantinople.

The war-cry of the Saracens, the Turks, the Arabs, " Allahu-akbar " (God is greater) sounded over the plains of the Danube through Hungary and Austria until, with the fierce chant, " La illaha ila allah wa Muhamed errasuhl allah " (There is no God but God, and Mohammed is His prophet), of which " Allahu-akbar " was the keynote, the desert tribes surged round the walls of the city of Central Europe, Vienna, the capital of the Holy Roman Empire of the German nation.

Defeat at Vienna. If Vienna fell, there would have been, humanly speaking, no hope for Christian Europe. Had it not been for the vigorous, but now decadent Polish nation, led by their noble knight, John Sobiesky, who defeated the Turks before the walls of the city on the 12th September, 1683, how different the history of Europe would have been. There would have been no seven years' war, no Frederick the Great, no French revolution, no Napoleon, no Waterloo or Trafalgar. The faith of Europe hung in the balance, but the

MOHAMMEDANISM AND SINUSSIISM 115

cyclone of religious war retreated, thanks to the bravery of the best of our Slavonic brethren.

The second continent which Islam desired was Asia. The crown of the Abassides of Persia had fallen soon after Mohammed established his faith in Arabia. Syria lay at his feet almost from the first; like a shoal of sharks the warriors of the Crescent swept into India and there gorged themselves on the wealth amassed during millenniums in that motherland of the Aryan race. But the wealth of India acted as a narcotic, and the fanatical enthusiasm waned. Their vanguard had got as far as the north of China and the islands of the East Indies, Sumatra and Java. The soft life in the south of Asia became the antidote against the Moslem conquest of that continent. *The Narcotic of India.*

The third and last continent of the old world in which Mohammedanism spread is Africa.

As stated at the commencement of this chapter, the conquest of the states of North Africa was accomplished in the first enthusiastic rush of the new-born Arab religion. It demolished the 1600 Christian bishoprics of Africa. It swept Christianity out of Tripoli, Tunis, Algiers, and Morocco. The Copts in Egypt only maintained themselves by fleeing to and hiding in the oases of the Libyan desert. Like a springtide wave Mohammedanism passed through the Sahara desert and up the Nile Valley, chasing Christianity out of the fruitful plains of the Gezira in the Eastern Sudan into the Alps of Abyssinia, the Switzerland of the Continent of Africa. Khartum *The Springtide wave of Islam in Africa.*

and Timbuktu were Mohammedan 700 years ago
Important Moslem States grew up along the
northern edge of the Sudan, States such as
Songhai, Hausaland, Bornu, Bagirmi, Kanem,
Wadai, Darfur, and Kordofan.

Let us look at the development of this conquest somewhat more minutely. It began in 638 A.D. Bonet-Maury points out that there were three periods in the conflict for Africa, though these periods may only be approximately dated. In the first, 638-1050 A.D., the Arabs, by rapid military conquest, overran the Mediterranean littoral from Egypt to Morocco, where the stubborn resistance of the Berbers, and especially discord among the Moslem rulers, prevented wider conquest until the tenth century. During the second period, from 1050-1750, Southern Morocco, the Sahara region, and the Western Sudan became Moslem, and the desire for conquest was, no doubt, provoked, in part as a reaction against the Christian Crusades. The third period—1750—to-day is that of the revival of Islam, and its spread through the Mahdi movement and the Derwish orders.

Egypt Fell. While Khalid carried the Moslem banner to victory in Syria and Western Persia, Amru-ibn-el-Aassi with equal furor invaded Egypt. Within two years (640 A.D.) Alexandria was taken, and Egypt became a dependency, like Syria and Chaldea. In 647 the armies moved westward, and within thirty years the victorious Moslems had reached the Atlantic Ocean, and were preparing to cross over into Spain. It is impossible to give here, even in summary, the story of these campaigns. The political victory was often an easy one, because the Christians were divided. In Egypt, one party, the Copts, welcomed the Mohammedan invaders as a means of deliverance from the orthodox Christian *Mukawkas*. However, they soon had abundant reason to regret it, and the religious victory of Islam was only partial, for there are still to-day in Egypt 1,000,000 Copts.

Abdulla invaded Tripoli in 647 A.D.; Akba penetrated to Mauritania in 677 A.D.; yet their bloody victories were largely valueless to Islam, because Christian civilisation fought here for its very life. It was not until 754 A.D. that, by the conversion of the Christian "infidels," tribute was abolished. Ibn Khaldun, the Moslem historian, states that those formerly Christians apostasised from Islam fourteen times. **Tripoli followed.**

The Arabs, in their later efforts at "conversion," whether for trade, conquest or slave-raids, entered Africa from three different sides. These three streams of Moslem immigration and conquest were as follows: From Egypt they went westward as far as Lake Chad; from the north-west of Africa they came down to Lake Chad and the Niger region; and from Zanzibar the slave dealers opened the way for Islam as far as the Great Lakes.

Mohammedan influence, in the first phase of its extension, stopped short of the desert zone, where there was a natural barrier from sea to sea, that was not easily overcome. The second

Westward Ho!

phase, from the eleventh to the seventeenth century, was inaugurated by the large Arab migrations from Egypt westwards. Numerous nomad tribes, with all their belongings, migrated to North-West Africa. Arab writers compute their numbers to have been as high as one million; others have estimated them at only 250,000. It is probable that other tribes soon followed along the road thus opened. This migration lasted from the middle of the eleventh to the thirteenth century, and resulted in Islam planting its banners in Songhai and Kanem, and on the East Coast.

According to Dr. Lenz,* the States of the Middle Niger have ever since remained the chief bulwark of Islam and the centre of an advanced civilisation. The history of Timbuktu, which was founded in 1077 by the Tuareck, shows, however, that the progress of Islam was not unattended by checks of one sort and another. Its domination over Kanem came somewhat later. As for the Fulah, they may or may not have been under its influence at this period.

Islam in East Africa.

The Arabs crossed the Red Sea in 740 A.D., but it is not until the ninth century that we hear of any extensive migrations, and not until the eleventh century, or the commencement of the twelfth, that they reached the confines of Abyssinia. Somal traditions lead one to infer that the Arabs also established themselves in their country and in other parts of East Africa, and warred against the Pagans in the south. The

* Timbuktu, Vol. II., p. 162.

Portuguese, at least, when they first reached this coast early in the sixteenth century, spoke of the powerful and inimical Mussulman rulers of the great "Adal" kingdom between Tajura and Cape Guardafui.

The Swaheli tribes were not converted until 1700 by the Oman traders of Zanzibar. The period of the greatest Arab immigration was that following the Crusades and, therefore, the missionary expansion of Islam in North Central Africa falls between the years 1095 and 1300. Islam crossed the Sahara about the year 1200. Its progress was slow, but irresistible. Islam in East Africa.

In the sixteenth and seventeenth centuries Islam extended its sway over other of the remaining countries of the Sudan. In Kordofan there are traces of its influence having been established as early as the fourteenth century, if not before. The evidence as regards Darfur and Wadai is uncertain : though as regards the latter, Barth considers that Islam had no footing there until 1640. The Bagirmi received Islam at the close of the sixteenth century, the Katsena in the seventeenth century, and the inhabitants of Kano a little later. But Barth states that the Hausa population remained Pagan until forced by the Fulah to make a public confession of their own faith. The influence of Islam during the second phase of its extension thus appears to have reached to the ninth parallel of north latitude, roughly speaking, and to have penetrated along the East Coast as far south as the Equator.

The third and last phase of the progress of

Third phase of Moslem progress.

Islam and of the Arab domination has had its chief development within the present century, and is due partly to the enterprise of the proselytising Fulah. In 1775 Othman, a Fulah of Gober, made a pilgrimage to Mecca, became imbued with the Wahabi desire for reform and conquest, returned and, transforming herdsmen into warriors, built up a strong Moslem empire at Sokoto. His power extended from the Atlantic to Lake Chad, and from the Benué river to the Sahara. His followers did not rest satisfied with founding agricultural colonies in the Central Sudan; they carried their conquests far to the south and east, and to the shores of the Atlantic. After conquest followed reconstruction. Through the warlike operations of the Fulah and the extension of commerce by the Hausa, the Mohammedans have now reached the Gulf of Guinea.

From 1835 to 1853 Mohammed Othman, of Mecca, was a zealous propagandist of Islam in Kordofan and Senaar, where many tribes were still pagan, and the order of Derwishes he founded still carries on his work. In West Africa the Kadiriya and Tijani orders have been active propagandists as traders and missionaries. From 1832 to 1847 Abd-ul-Kader, poet and statesman, and a devout Algerian Moslem, strove to recall the Arabs of North Africa to the duty of preaching Islam, and a little later the Mahdist movement in the Egyptian Sudan extended the faith with fire and sword against the "infidels," and lukewarm believers.

But the latest and strongest Moslem missionary force in Africa is that of the Sinussi brotherhood, the Jesuits of Islam.

We have seen the initiation of a war of half a millennium, a war for the backbone of the Continent of Africa; a war waged between the brave independent fetish worshippers in the mountains of Marra, of Adamawa, of Mandara, Bauchi, the Murchison Hills, the swamps of the Sudd region and the middle Shari, on the one hand, and the mounted armies of the Sultanates of the North Sudan on the other. *The Jesuits of Islam.*

> "Allah herrschet in Dar Fur,
> Und es drohet Todesstrafe
> Jedem, der zu dem entthronten,
> Alten Heidengotte betet.
>
> Zu dem Heidengotte Kalge ;
> Wessen Hand zu ihm sich aufreckt,
> Ueber den mit Grabesdunkel
> Fällt der Schatten Alba Kuras."

Slowly Islam had spread down the East Coast of Africa; slowly it penetrated into the Congo valley, to South Africa, and, in our days, to West Africa. But in the heart of the Continent advance was impossible.

Now all this is changed. What Mohammedanism failed to accomplish in its own strength Christian Europe is assisting it to do. We have brought the Pagan tribes in Central Africa into subjection; we have established peace; we have built high roads, and we protect the Moslem trader, the Moslem pilgrim and the Moslem

The Sign of the Night.

teacher. Yea! and we go so far as to send Moslem administrators to the Pagans. Unless in some way or other this advance of Islam is checked, we shall see the faith of the Crescent—the Sign of the Night—dominate the Dark Continent.

In Europe it was the sword of the brave, in Asia it was the gold of the weak before which Islam went down. In Central Africa the Pagans have not the gold of Asia, though they have the bravery of medieval Europe. But a stronger than Mohammedanism has come, the white children of Light. They have roped the arms of the warrior tribes of Ethiopia in the bonds of peace, and the fighting remnants are now directly and indirectly handed over by European Governments to the spiritual slavery of Islam.

Sir Alfred Sharpe, Governor of Nyassaland, in the course of an interview with Reuter's representative, draws attention to the startling progress of Mohammedanism in Nyassaland. "Twenty years ago, when I first knew Nyassaland," he says, "Mohammedanism was almost non-existent. Since then it has spread greatly, particularly during the last eight or ten years." He adds that all through Taoland there is a mosque and a Moslem teacher in almost every village.

Advance of the Crescent in Nyassaland

That these people might have been drawn from heathenism to Christianity instead of to Mohammedanism seems to be proved by the fact that, according to Sir Alfred, the tribes to the west of Lake Nyassa have taken up Christianity with equal enthusiasm. The Moslem success is disquieting from a political as well as from a religious point of view. "The movement," states the Governor, "is as yet quite harmless, but it is, of course, always true that Mohammedanism is, and must be, more or less opposed to European influence."

In little over 100 years Mohammedanism has spread all over the Sierra Leone Protectorate, and is advancing rapidly. Fifty years ago there were less than 2,000 Mahommedans in the colony; to-day there are 10,000 in Freetown alone. *In Sierra Leone.*

Bishop Gwynne, of Khartum, states that the advance of Mohammedanism in the Anglo-Egyptian Sudan is so rapid that Christian Missions will either have to occupy the land within the next ten years, or the tribes will have become Mohammedan. Mohammedanism at the present moment spreads like weeds. Every Mohammedan is a religious propagandist, but every Englishman is not a Christian missionary. *In the Anglo-Egyptian Sudan.*

Much of our modern literature disseminates ideas as to the Mohammedan religion that must look very quaint to a student of history, geography, and political economy.

Hall Caine's book, "The White Prophet," and Marmaduke Pickthall's "Said, the Fisherman," and "Champion of Christendom," bring before the public at large an aspect of Mohammedanism that is not founded on fact, and that leaves behind in the reader's mind impressions of the glory of Islam which are not borne out by experience and the past. *"The White Prophet."*

The European who sees the Mahommedan devotee at prayer in the railway-stations of Egypt and in the highways and byways, receives the impression that the Moslem who so thoroughly believes in his religion must surely be a good man. He will think somewhat differently should he happen, in Tripoli or certain parts of Asia Minor and Syria, to get into the way of the Mohammeds, the Alis, the Abdullahs, who have little or no restraint placed upon them by European Christian police.

If the Christian admirer of Mohammedanism has his wife or mother treated the way Christian European women have been treated, not once, but many times, by the religious Moslem in the near East; if he has seen the pious Abu-Bekar expectorate on his wife and call his mother " a daughter of a dog," I hardly think that he will be much impressed in the days to come by the prayers of Abu-Bekar or Muhamed.

Ignorant and fanatical. The Moslem may be clothed in rags, he may be as unclean as possible, as ignorant as the donkey he drives, yet he will despise the Christian, whom he calls a pig or " a son of a dog." And those Moslems in the interior of North Africa who may never have seen a Christian before are the worst. It is not familiarity that breeds contempt, but it is the religion, the intolerance, the pride which is independent of social standing that forms the foundation of Islam. The Sermon on the Mount of Jesus Christ, and the teaching of the Koran, and especially that part of the Koran written in Medina, are further apart than the

Poles. The Sermon on the Mount inspires humility and meekness, but Islam is not meek nor humble. Christians were slave raiders in spite of the teaching of Christ, but Moslems were and are slave raiders because of the teaching of the Koran. *Further apart than the Poles.*

The Suras (chapters) of the Koran written in Mecca breathe gentleness and respect for others. But the Suras of Medina, the latter Suras, are proud, inflated, immoral, inhuman. They are anti-Christian, denying the foundation truths of our most holy faith. The Mecca Suras are sound, and laid the foundations for the Moslem Empire, but the corroding influence of the Medina Suras will destroy that Empire. And while one would hardly go so far as to call Muhamed "the first-born son of Satan," as Luther did, yet I think one is justified in holding that to the eternal truth, "there is no God but God," has been linked an eternal lie, "and Muhamed is the prophet of God." And truth mixed with error is the strength of that creed. *An eternal truth linked with an eternal lie.*

The Mohammedan conquest was unlike the conquest of the Christian religion, which, in the third century after Christ, through humility and religious fervour, had succeeded in vanquishing paganism in the lands round the Mediterranean. With Islam it was not the religious fervour finding expression in love and humility, nor was it truth, but bloodshed, fire and death, the besom of war which swept the lands of the near East, and North Africa, of the faith of Christ and nine-tenths of their population. *The Besom of War.*

The political power of the Crescent began to wane in the middle of the last century. The sword of Moslem fanaticism had rested in its sheath, the days of the green flag of the holy war lay in the half-forgotten past. People in Egypt and North Africa had made friends with the once despised "Christian dogs." Ramadan, the month of fasting, was little observed, intoxicants freely indulged in, and the Mecca pilgrimage and the mosques neglected.

Sinussi. It was at this time that the Mohammedan reform movement, Sinussi-ism, came into being.

Muhamed Ben-Ali-Es-Sinussi, the leader of this reformation, was born at Mostaganem in 1796. He was an educated man, went to college at Fez, the University of Morocco, and after having finished his studies, when thirty-four years of age traversed the States of North Africa, and went on pilgrimage to Mecca. Devout in his prayers, devoted with heart and soul to the faith of Muhamed, he was a strong man, a natural born leader.

He had been a short while in Mecca when he founded his first Institution, the "Sauwija" of Djebel-Abu-Koubeis, not far from the Kaaba. There was no distinctive feature in his teaching except intense earnestness. Prayers which had to be said five times a day lasted about an hour each time. During Ramadan, fasting was a *sine qua non*. All members of the Sinussi Society must assist their brethren, and in that sense, like the Freemasons, are held together in strong solidarity. To train teachers, control the education of the young, and instil into the boys a reverence for the Koran and a perfect knowledge of that book was held by Sinussi the best way to bring Mohammedans back to the original powerful faith of the prophet.

In 1850 Sidi Muhamed began his journey back from Mecca towards the west, whence he had come. He went through Arabia and Egypt, and after having passed Siwa he found a great welcome in the oasis of Jarbub, in the interior of Barbary, south-east of Bengazi. A number of years he lived in this oasis, taught and instructed others, and from time to time dispatched his oldest pupils to become, in their turn, teachers. *Sidi Muhamed.*

It grew into a custom for his followers to add to their name the name of Sinussi, and thus mark their adherence to the new sect. With remarkable rapidity, recommended by the simplicity and the severity of its tenets, the Sinussi denomination spread.

And with it commenced a new era of Moslem peaceful proselytising among the Pagans of Central Africa. The mosques in Tripoli came into the hands of Sinussi; a number of the oases of the Sahara were converted to the new faith. Since 1856 a representative of the Sinussi movement was maintained at the court of the Sultan of Turkey in Constantinople, and it was at one time thought that Sultan Abdul Hamid was very much under the control of the Sinussi ambassador. This is certain,—that the members of the Sinussi brotherhood did not pay taxes to the Turks in the Cyrenaika. *Proselytising.*

Sinussi's son, Sidi-el-Mahdi, who was born in 1844, succeeded in the leadership of the new movement. The young high priest was, in many respects, not as wise as his father, and the society did not develop as fast as previously. The tables were turned in Constantinople, and instead of Sinussi dominating the decisions on the Golden Horn, Sidi-el-Mahdi became afraid that the Turkish Government or some of the Christian nations of Europe would come to Jarbub, his headquarters, and there legislate for him.

Headquarters changed. In 1895 the headquarters of the Sinussi movement were removed from Jarbub to Kufra, an oasis in the Sahara halfway to the Sudan. Kufra has never been explored by Europeans, and the only white man who attempted to visit it, Dr. Rohlfs, in 1883, only escaped with his life by mounting a running camel, leaving all his possessions behind, and riding day and night northward till he reached the Mediterranean.

About this same time the head of the Sinussi sect fell out with the Sultan of Turkey. The former insisted on having all the trade across the Sahara taken away from the old desert high road, Lake Chad, Murzuk, Tripoli, and turned into a new channel, Wadai, Borku, Kufra, Jarbub, and Bengazi. The Tripolitan traders, one would have thought, would have objected to seeing their trade route diverted, but as they were all followers of Sinussi it appears that they were perfectly satisfied.

I have been told repeatedly in Tripoli as as well in the Libyan desert and in the

MOHAMMEDANISM AND SINUSSIISM

Sudan regions, that a Sinussi could travel from the Sudan to the Mediterranean without any money or food supply, simply living on the hospitality of his co-religionists. There are also said to be Sinussi monasteries along the road from time to time where any Sinussi traveller or pilgrim would be welcome.

Twelve years ago one of the Sinussi leaders, Sidi-Mohamed-Sunni, went on a commercial mission to Wadai and Kanem to arrange for the trade with these Sudan States.

When some ten years ago I was hospitably received by a Sinussi chief in the village of Moot in the oasis of Dachla in the Libyan desert, the host when asked why the Sinussis disliked the Europeans, said the Sinussis did not desire to war against the Christians as long as they were not attacked. "Leave us alone, and we will leave you alone," seemed to be the principle of their policy.

"Leave us alone."

During the later days of the Derwish rule in Khartum the Khalifa sent to Sinussi and asked him if he would agree to become his successor.

Sinussi replied, "Who are you, son of a dog? I know you not."

Sinussi was a fanatical religious leader, while the Khalifa was a blood-thirsty robber chief.

Sidi-el-Mahdi left the oasis of Kufra eleven years ago, in 1899. I was at that time travelling in the southern parts of the Libyan desert, and messengers from Egypt arrived with the information that Sinussi might be expected at any time, but instead of crossing the desert and mountains towards the east, he went further south to the mountain regions of Borku and Tibesti, and there he died in 1902.

As far as I have been able to learn, the Sinussi movement is controlled to-day by a Council of Elders in Borku, whose head is Sidi Ahmed Sherif-es-Sinussi. I have met with members of the Sinussi sect in Egypt, in the Libyan desert, in Tripoli, in Tunis, in Sierra Leone, in Northern Nigeria, in Adamawa, in the Shari Chad Protectorate, and in the Eastern Sudan, showing over what vast area this movement has spread already.

Sinussi-ism.

The largest mosque in Sierra Leone belongs to the Sinussi people; the largest mosque in Tripoli also belongs to them. There are Sinussi mosques in Morocco, in Algiers, and Tunis numbered by hundreds, if not thousands. The Sinussi movement is not a political movement but a religious one. It has, therefore, no fighting organisation, but thousands of rifles, which have been smuggled into Africa by Italians through Tripoli, are now in the hands of the Sinussi people, and might, under certain conditions, be used against the Christian Infidels. The most powerful Sinussi leader of to-day is, without doubt, Sultan Sinussi-Ndele, who rules over a country about as large as France, and is one of the strongest independent Central African chiefs.

When Sidi Barrani was sent, in 1898, to Kanem and the other countries of the Lake Chad region, no representative of the European powers had reached the shores of that lake, and but a

MOHAMMEDANISM AND SINUSSIISM 131

very few explorers had seen its waters. Three years Sidi Barrani spent in persuading the Tuarecks of Air and the Tubus between Borku and Chad to attempt the commercial conquest of the Sudan States. A new caravan route was, therefore, opened through Borku to Kufra, where it joined the route through Wadai. The Sinussis became, at this time, the greatest slave traders of Africa, and when the French attempted to dislodge them from their strongholds in Kanem, very serious fighting ensued, but in the end they were driven from Bir-Alali and compelled to retreat, in 1901, to Borku.

An important French expedition was sent there in 1907, and this resulted in considerably adding to our knowledge of the actual strength and disposal of the Sinussi forces and resources. **The French Expedition.**

This expedition, in April, 1907, traversed Borku, and, in a great fight at Ain-Galakka, defeated the Sinussis. We may hear at any moment that a French expedition has succeeded in crossing the mountain oases of Ennedi and Kufra, thus reaching the Mediterranean. The indomitable energy, enterprise, and heroism displayed by many of these French officers is something that one cannot but admire. With hardly any subsidies from France, a few dozen Frenchmen have forced their way into the very centre of the Sudan, coming from Algiers in the North, from the Senegal in the West, and from the lower Congo. They have established their Shari-Chad Protectorate with practically no European support; they have faced the Sinussi

movement; they have beaten the Sultan of Ngaumdere in German Adamawa; they have broken Rabba, have vanquished the Sultan of Bagirmi, and utterly routed the Waidains. La Gloire is a very real thing to a French soldier of fortune in Central Africa.

With the words of Silva White, an authority on the geography of Africa, I will close :—

"Without exactly foretelling a crusade or a crescentade in Africa, it is obvious that these antagonistic elements are bound to clash wherever rivalries of territorial expansion may exist. Africa, indeed, bids fair to become the chief, if not the last, battlefield of Cross and Crescent."

Heathenism in the Sudan

"Only like souls I see the folk thereunder,
  Bound who should conquer,—slaves
    who should be kings;
  Hearing their one hope with an empty
    wonder,
  Sadly contented with a show of things."

CHAPTER VIII

THE animistic religions of Africa may be divided, like all the religions of the world, into three parts, and form the rudimentary basis for the more developed creeds of the East, and the monotheistic religions of which Christianity, containing the perfect revelation, is the highest form. The three divisions are the following. *Animistic Religions in Africa.*

Firstly, we have the worship of the heavenly bodies, the sun, moon and stars, and the evolution of it, day and night, light and darkness, good and evil, Ormuz and Ahriman; secondly, ancestral worship, the worship of spirits, demons, and the Lord of all the spirits; and thirdly, the worship of creatures, animals, (with which is connected the trans-migration of souls), trees; forces of nature that lead to Nirvana.

The last is the most rudimentary class. We find it in the worship of crocodiles in Egypt, of trees amongst the Anglo-Saxons, of wells and groves amongst the Greeks, of serpents, of lions and other wild animals, of the cow, monkeys and elephants in India; and it culminates in Buddhism.

The second class has its examples in the ancestral worship in China, and in the Central African belief in a supreme God, the combination of all the departed spirits.

The Fore-shadowing. In the first, we have the sun worship of Ra in Egypt, of fire amongst the Persians, of the new moon and the sun among the Celts; and it culminates in the Moslem faith, of which the Crescent is the sign and symbol. This first class contains the foreshadowing of the perfect divine revelation in Jesus Christ, the Light of the world, the Sun of Righteousness.

A few examples of these different branches of religious thought in Africa may not be without interest. At Wukari, in Northern Nigeria, there is a pool inhabited by crocodiles. A good deal of the drinking-water is drawn from it, and the women of the place congregate at it to wash their clothes and fill their water-pots. I have seen the women stand amongst the crocodiles with perfect unconcern. None of these crocodiles would touch a human being. They are held by the natives to be inhabited by spirits, and thought to be divine. At certain periods lambs and goats are sacrificed to them, so I was told.

Dogeri's Transformation. It is a common belief amongst the people that certain individuals are able to transform themselves into wild beasts, hyenas, leopards, or lions. It was generally held at Wasé that my hunter, named Dogeri, was a man who could, if he so wished, at any time transform himself into a hyena. And much amusement was caused by my insisting one day that Dogeri should transform

himself, and take the form of the fore-mentioned beast. His excuse, of course, was that only at night time had he the power to do so, and then only if no other human being was present. Dogeri was a great *ju-ju* man in his own country, and had a checkered career behind him. Being of Yergum extraction, he had later become the executioner of the chief of Wasé, and then developed into a witch-doctor, and finally ended as my hunter. He frequently expressed his desire to become a Christian and worship the great God of the white man, but his professions were not always sincere.

For the second class we have the Dodo worship in the Central Sudan. While Dodo amongst certain tribes is only a hobgoblin with which to frighten women and children, in most of the tribes Dodo represents the combination of all the departed spirits. To the Dodo groves, specially enclosed, shady, rocky places, the natives bring regularly pots of millet beer and flour as food for the All-soul. Over the graves of the dead, chickens are usually sacrificed and their blood poured on the fresh mould in honour of Dodo. If a man desires Dodo to watch over his field, he will drive a short stick into the ground in the corner of it, hang an earthenware-pot on the top, and tie the wing of a bird to the stick. There seems to be some connection between birds' feathers and Dodo, but I have not been able to find out the reason why.

Dodo Worship.

All the pagans of Central Africa are afraid of the darkness, like children at home.

The shadows are peopled with brownies and spooks.

Desert-born strength. It is a remarkable fact that when on my first visit into the Sahara, I was left alone for hours in the desert mountains more than a hundred miles away from the nearest water, where silence reigned, silence that could be felt, where there was no creeping insect, no blade of grass, no breath of wind, an eerie feeling of life unseen seemed to come over me, a feeling which even in my childhood days I had never known. The spirits congregate, as the Bible says, in desert places. In wrestling with unseen powers, spiritual leaders have acquired their strength in the deserts.

The highest class of religious beliefs is founded on the worship of the heavenly bodies. The Central Africans who believe in the principle of good and evil, a good spirit and an evil spirit, all direct their worship towards the evil spirit. And very reasonably too, for the good spirit will not hurt them, but they must propitiate the evil one. Thus they sacrifice black fowls and animals to the powers of darkness.

Heathenism's superlative. The superlative of heathenism is Islam, in which the devotee five times a day bows to the dust facing in the direction of his temple, the Kaaba, and the holiest of it, the black stone which fell from heaven. The ceremonies of Islam are, many of them, connected with the night. The Mohammedan fasts during the day, but feasts during the night in Ramadan. His ark of covenant is a dark black stone, his sign of victory the crescent of the night.

HEATHENISM IN THE SUDAN

The three-fold division of religious beliefs is founded on the tri-partite nature of men; some growing out of the physical, others out of the mental, and others again out of the soul life of man.

"The Central African religions are Pantheistic, Polytheistic and Monotheistic. Much of the Pantheism in Central Africa would be called at home a philosophy of religion. The great Spirit of the Bantu is a spirit formed by adding all the departed spirits together; and in these spirits part of the All-Spirit is omnipresent, that is to say, there are spirits in all countries. In worshipping the Great Spirit the natives usually approach him through their departed relatives. There is a distinct belief among the natives that when death supervenes the soul leaves the body.

Philosophy of Religion.

"An ancient philosopher was asked by his friends, when he was dying, what they should do with him after his death. 'All very well,' was the reply, 'if you can catch me.'"

"There seems to be a difference of opinion as to whether a spirit can be killed, and some believe that during the transmigration of soul, when the human spirit enters a snake and the snake is killed, the spirit dies. Others again believe that if the snake is killed the human spirit is liberated. The spirits of all deceased men and women, with the exception of wizards and witches, become objects of religious homage. There are, therefore, among the natives as many gods almost as there are dead. All cannot be worshipped, and, therefore, a selection has to be made. The people naturally turn to their dead relatives and amongst those they worship, either the great dead chiefs or their own fathers and grandfathers."

Carlyle, in "Heroes and Hero Worship," points out, quite correctly, that the old heathen gods of Europe were originally human beings endowed with exceptional intelligence and physical strength. Amongst the Central African tribes there are family gods similar to the Penates of the Romans, village gods, gods inhabiting special localities, and superior deities. There are gods of mountains. There is supposed to be a god living on the top of the Kamerun Mountain, another on Mount Kenia. There are gods of lakes, rivers, and forests. There is a god of rain, and a god of thunder and lightning. Then there is a god of famine and a god of harvest, to whom the natives chant a hymn imploring him on behalf of their crops. This harvest god, called in British Central Africa Chitowe, " may become a child or a young woman. In his disguise he visits villages, and tells whether the coming year will bring food or famine. He receives their hospitality, but throws the food over his shoulder without eating it."

Penates.

"Another god of the same district is Npambe, who is the god of lightning, and as lightning in Central Africa is usually connected with rain, he is the god of rain. The latter god of the Central Africans usually lives on the top of the highest mountain in the region. Thus the chief god of the Adamawa pagans lives on the top of Mount Atlantic."

HEATHENISM IN THE SUDAN

Mary Kingsley, who in her book, "Travels in West Africa," has several chapters on fetishism, tells us that stalking the wild West African idea is one of the most charming pursuits in the world. Quite apart from the intellect, it has a sporting interest, for its pursuit is as beset with difficulty and danger as grizzly-bear hunting. She tells us in these chapters that she was only on the threshold. She states, "*Ich weiss nicht all doch viel ist mir bekannt.*" (I know not all, but much is known to me), as Faust has said. She relates a story of the creation as extant among the Cabindas. "God made at first all men black—He always does in the African story—and then He went across a great river, and called man to follow Him, and the wisest and the boldest and the best plunged into the great river and crossed it; and the water washed them white. So they are the ancestors of the white man. Others were afraid too much, and said ' No, we are comfortable here. We have our dances and our tom-toms, and plenty to eat. We won't risk it, we will stay here.' And they remained in the old place, and from them came the black men. But to this day the white men come to the black men, saying, 'Come, it is better over here.'"

<small>Stalking the African Idea.</small>

<small>Why are the Negroes black?</small>

She goes on to say that she warns people in general that their minds require protection when they send them stalking the savage idea through the tangled forests, the dark caves, the swamps and the fogs of the Ethiopian intellect.

"They regard their god as the creator of man,

plants, animals, and the earth, and they hold that having made them, he takes no further interest in the affair. But not so the crowd of spirits with which the universe is peopled, they take only too much interest, and the Bantu wishes they would not, and is perpetually saying so in his prayers, a large percentage whereof amounts to 'Go away, we don't want you.' 'Come not into this house, this village, or its plantations.' He knows from experience that the spirits pay little heed to these objurgations, and as they are people who must be attended to, he develops a cult whereby they may be managed, used, and understood. This cult is what we call witchcraft.

<small>Propitiating the Spirits.</small>

"As I am not here writing a complete work on Fetish, I will leave Nzam on one side, and turn to the inferior spirits. These are almost all malevolent; sometimes they can be coaxed into having creditable feelings, like generosity and gratitude, but you can never trust them. No, not even if you are yourself a well-established medicine man. Indeed, they are particularly dangerous to medicine men, just as lions are to lion tamers, and many a professional gentleman in the full bloom of his practice gets eaten up by his own particular familiar, which he has to keep in his own inside when he has not sent it off into other people's."

"Dr. Nassau classified the different spirits believed in by the native Central African in the following way:—

"1. Human disembodied spirits—*Manu*.

HEATHENISM IN THE SUDAN 143

"2. Vague beings, well described by our words ghosts—*Amambo*.

"3. Beings something like dryads, who resent intrusion into their territory, on to their rock, past their promontory, or tree. When passing the residence of one of these beings, the traveller must go by silently, or with some cabalistic invocation, with bowed or bared head, and deposit some symbol of an offering or tribute, even if it be only a pebble. You occasionally come across great trees that have fallen across a path that have quite little heaps of pebbles, small shells, &c., upon them, deposited by previous passers-by. This class is called *Ombwiri*.

Tribute Offerings.

"4. Beings who are agents in causing sickness, and either aid or hinder human plans—*Mionde*.

"5. There seems to be, the Doctor says, another class of spirits, somewhat akin to the ancient Lares and Penates, who especially belong to the household, and descend by inheritance with the family. In their honour are *secretly* kept a bundle of finger, or other bones, nail-clippings, eyes, brains, skulls, particularly the lower jaws, called in M'pongwe *oginga*, accumulated from deceased members of successive generations."

Dr. Nassau says "secretly," and he refers to this custom being existent in non-cannibal tribes. Miss Kingsley saw bundles of this character among the cannibal Fans, and among the non-cannibal Adooma, openly hanging up in the thatch of the sleeping apartment.

Spirits in Animals.

"6. He also says there may be a sixth class, which may, however, only be a function of any of the other classes, namely, those that enter into any animal body, generally a leopard. Sometimes the spirits of living human beings do this, and the animal is then guided by human intelligence, and will exercise its strength for the purposes of its temporary human possessor. In other cases it is a non-human soul that enters into the animal.

"The Igalwa and other tribes will allow no one but a trusted friend to do their hair, and bits of nails and hair are carefully burnt or thrown away into a river; and blood, even that from a small cut or a fit of nose-bleeding, is most carefully covered up and stamped out if it has fallen on the earth. The underlying idea regarding blood is, of course, the old one that the blood is the life.

Life means a Spirit.

"The life in Africa means a spirit, hence the liberated blood is the liberated spirit, and liberated spirits are always whipping into people who do not want them.

"Charms are made for every occupation and desire in life, loving, hating, buying, selling, fishing, planting, travelling, hunting, &c., and although they are usually in the forms of things filled with a mixture in which the spirit nestles, yet there are other kinds; for example, a great love charm is made of the water the lover has washed in, and this, mingled with the drink of the loved one, is held to soften the hardest heart.

"Some kinds of charms, such as those to prevent your getting drowned, shot, seen by elephants, &c., are worn on a bracelet or necklace. A new-born child starts with a health-knot tied round the wrist, neck, or loins, and throughout the rest of its life its collection of charms goes on increasing. This collection does not, however, attain inconvenient dimensions, owing to the failure of some of the charms to work.

Charms.

"That is the worst of charms and prayers. The thing you wish of them may, and frequently does, happen in a strikingly direct way, but other times it does not. In Africa this is held to arise from the bad character of the spirits; their gross ingratitude and fickleness. You may have taken every care of a spirit for years, given it food and other offerings that you wanted for yourself, wrapped it up in your cloth on chilly nights, and gone cold, put it in the only dry spot in the canoe, and so on, yet after all this, the wretched thing will be capable of being got at by your rival or enemy, and lured away, leaving you only the case it once lived in.

"Finding, we will say, that you have been upset and half-drowned, and your canoe-load of goods lost three times in a week, that your paddles are always breaking, and the amount of snags in the river and so on is abnormal, you judge that your canoe-charm has stopped. Then you go to the medicine-man who supplied you with it, and complain. He says it was a perfectly good charm when he sold it you, and he never

"A big curio" for a white man.

had any complaints before, but he will investigate the affair; when he has done so, he either says the spirit has been lured away from the home he prepared for it by incantations and presents from other people, or that he finds the spirit is dead; it has been killed by a more powerful spirit of its class, which is in the pay of some enemy of yours. In all cases the little thing you kept the spirit in is no use now, and only fit to sell to a white man as 'a big curio'! and the sooner you let him have sufficient money to procure you a fresh and still more powerful spirit—necessarily more expensive—the safer it will be for you, particularly as your misfortunes distinctly point to some one being desirous of your death. You, of course, grumble, but seeing the thing in his light you pay up, and the medicine man goes busily to work with incantations, dances, looking into mirrors or basins of still water, and concoctions of messes to make you a new protecting charm.

"Human eyeballs, particularly of white men, are a great charm. Dr. Nassau says he has known graves rifled for them. This, I fancy, is to secure the 'man that lives in your eyes' for the service of the village, and naturally the white man, being regarded as a superior being, would be of high value if enlisted into its service. A similar idea of the possibility of gaining possession of the spirit of a dead man obtains among the Negroes, and the heads of important chiefs in the Calabar districts are usually cut from the body on burial and kept

"The man that lives in your eyes."

secretly for fear the head, and thereby the spirit, of the dead chief, should be stolen from the town. If it were stolen it would be not only a great advantage to its new possessor, but a great danger to the chief's old town, because he would know all the peculiar *ju-ju* relating to it. For each town has a peculiar one, kept exceedingly secret, in addition to the general *ju-jus*, and this secret one would then be in the hands of the new owners of the spirit. It is for similar reasons that brave General MacCarthy's head was treasured by the Ashantees, and so on.

"Charms are not all worn upon the body, some go to the plantations, and are hung there, ensuring an unhappy and swift end for the thief who comes stealing. Some are hung round the bows of the canoe, others over the doorway of the house, to prevent evil spirits from coming in—a sort of tame watch-dog spirits.

"The entrances to the long street-shaped villages are frequently closed with a fence of saplings, and this sapling fence you will see hung with fetish charms to prevent spirits from entering the village, and sometimes in addition to charms you will see the fence wreathed with leaves and flowers. Bells are frequently hung on these fences, but I do not fancy ever for fetish reasons. At Ndorko, on the Rembwé, there were many guards against spirit visitors, but the bell, which was carefully hung so that you could not pass through the gateway without ringing it, was a guard against thieves and human enemies only.

Village Charm Protection.

"Frequently a sapling is tied horizontally near the ground across the entrance. Dr. Nassau could not tell me why, but says it must never be trodden on. When the smallpox, a dire pestilence in these regions, is raging, or when there is war, these gateways are sprinkled with the blood of sacrifices, and for the payments of heavy blood fines, &c., goats and sheep are kept. They are rarely eaten for ordinary purposes, and these West Coast Africans have all a perfect horror of the idea of drinking milk, holding this custom to be a filthy habit, and saying so in unmitigated language.

"The villagers eat the meat of the sacrifices, that having nothing to do with the sacrifice to the spirits, which is the blood, for the blood is the life.*

"The religious excitements of the indigenous negro tribes point to the universal belief in spirits, if not in a divinity, and in a future life of some sort. 'Some believe,' says Ratzel, 'that the soul (breath) dies with the man, but the spirit (shadow) goes into the earth, and returns from thence. Burial places are therefore sacred. Gross superstitions, of course, exist. The world to them is full of spirits. There is a spirit in everything, whether animate or inanimate objects. Thus animals are supposed to possess the souls of men, and the worship of snakes, crocodiles,

Belief in Spirits.

* Care must be taken not to confuse with sacrifices (propitiations of spirits), the killing of men and animals as offerings to the souls of deceased persons.

HEATHENISM IN THE SUDAN

cocks, is not uncommon. The wholesale practice of human sacrifices, wives, relatives, or slaves to the deceased—or even subordinate chiefs—was one of the main causes of depopulation in Africa, while ' smelling out ' of witches and obnoxious individuals was another."

A. Silva White, in his " Development of Africa," says on page 87, " the character of the negro in his primitive state is that of the overgrown child; his superficial, impressionable nature is the cause of many virtues and failings in him. He is vain, self-indulgent, demonstrative, and theatrical, but he has 'a good heart.' Livingstone, whose experience of the negro character was unrivalled, appears to have come to the conclusion that after all the negro is no better and no worse than the rest of the sons of men. And indeed we Europeans appear to the unsophisticated savages a most immoral and wicked people. Their judgment of us is, in fact, crippled by much the same limitations that prejudice our judgment of them. The negro is, in short, an untrained child of nature, and want of self-control or of ' character '—generally the products of civilisation—naturally accentuate his failings."

Overgrown Children.

Only those who have lived with him learn his many excellent qualities of heart and mind. Mons. Elise Réclus, the eminent geographer, gives the negroes of Africa a good character. He says they are docile and faithful, and have many " feminine " characteristics; they are timid, curious, jealous, and coquettish, braggarts, lovers of secrets, fond of petty quarrels, and speedy reconciliations.

Moreover, they are satisfied to obey, and to be sacrificed for those who oppress and ill-use them.

The outskirts of civilisation. Lying and stealing come natural to an oppressed people, and it is true these failings are acquired in an extraordinary degree on the outskirts of civilisation. In South Africa this phenomenon has been most strikingly exemplified. Our contact with the native races has resulted in their deterioration, for they have learned our vices and not our virtues. Only the Kaffir and Zulu tribes have been able to withstand our blighting influence.

The stamina and vitality of the negro race must be very great since it has withstood for centuries such devasting scourges as the slave trade, incessant tribal wars, barbarous practices (human sacrifices, ordeals, witchcraft), and unchecked disease. As an agriculturist, the negro is unsurpassed. He is more efficient in this respect than the weaker Coolie or the more intelligent Chinaman. His dexterity is remarkable in the practice of any new handicraft. His precocity in book-learning is equally great. Up to the age of ten coloured children surpass white children in quickness of acquisition, but remain woefully behind between the ages of ten and twenty. There are, of course, exceptions to this rule. The negro is capable of great endurance. He is capable of work, too—of any amount of work—as a *free* man,

HEATHENISM IN THE SUDAN

but as a slave he will render no more than his taskmaster exacts.

The bonds of family relationship are very strong in the African. The love of the mother for her child is as potent a passion in the negress as among her European sisters, and her influence in the family (the tongue being the most effective weapon), is much greater than that of its nominal head, the father. The man performs the work which is most fitted to his strength, whilst the woman is employed on tasks requiring skill and endurance. Like most natural peoples, the natives of Africa are very "musical," that is to say, they have a highly-developed sense of rhythm and noise, and indulge in it *ad nauseam*. The negro truly loves to talk; to talk and to argue, and is an astute diplomatist, as many Europeans have found to their cost. [Family bonds.]

Tacitus, in his "Germania," characterises the Germans as lazy, happy-go-lucky, easy-living people, who lay all day on their bare skins. Silva White, drawing his conclusions from many writings, says the negro is a child of nature; he loves a life of easy and self-indulgence—just like our forefathers.

In the following let me present a few pictures drawn by missionaries among the heathen in the Sudan, showing habits and customs of the tribes:—

"The people, as a rule, do not marry very young. The young men and maidens live in their father's houses, doing their share of the work, and

Harvest feasting.

working in the fields until the corn is ripe. When the harvest is gathered in, a time of merrymaking begins, and each house has its fête, which, more often than not, develops into a drinking bout. (Just like the old Saxons).

"As the sun is going down, the people from the neighbouring houses begin to assemble, and when the master of ceremonies arrives, armed with a drum, the few who are present arrange themselves in a circle around him, and, *follow-my-leader style*, commence slowly walking round and round with a species of dance, better described as a wriggle, while our drummer friend keeps up a constant tum-a-tum-tum, and the whole party shouts a kind of hoarse chant. Presently a new arrival appears, dressed up in his feathers and fur, his hair shaved into some fantastic shape, and picked out with vermilion, while he carries his spear or battle-axe. The latter may come in handy if a brawl arises. On his legs are iron anklets, carrying loose rings which jingle as he moves, or he may be the proud possessor of a grass harp, or a one-stringed fiddle.

"His fellows call upon him to join them, and if he has any clothes he divests himself of them, knowing the dance may cause considerable exertion. Then, with a piercing yell, with his battle-axe raised as though he were about to dash into the fray, he rushes at the ring, stopping just in time to avoid a catastrophe, and joins in the chant and wriggle as though nothing had happened.

"So they continue, hour after hour, the ring ever expanding with the additions of men and women, the chant getting hoarser, and the yells coarser, as the dust rises, and the moon creeps high into the sky.

"Periodically the noise stops, only to be renewed with fresh vigour after the native beer has been handed round by the old women of the house. Late into the night the carousal continues, till some fall down to sleep off the effects of drink, others wend their way homewards across the silent bush.

"In the morning they sleep, and when they do turn out it is with aching limbs, and a voice which is scarcely audible.

"This is pleasure! and in the height of the season may continue for several nights in succession. Not that we, as a nation, can find fault with this heathen folly, for, truly, that would be a case of 'the pot calling the kettle black.'

Heathen pleasure.

"It is at these parties that the young people exchange their first fond glances. The father is acquainted with the affair, and later, perhaps, the youth will make him a present of cloth, grain, or a sheep. To win his lady's love seems to be an arduous task. 'The course of true love never did run smooth.' He takes with him a number of friends from his father's house and clan, and sets off to the house of the bride. Here the process of serenading takes the form of a feast as depicted above, the lover being the master of ceremonies, and leading the chanting. But, instead of stopping his song when all the rest have fallen out or gone home, he is obliged to go wailing on, right through the night till early morning, when the muses are satisfied, and he can give rest and drink to his parched throat.

The Sign of Peace.
"Exactly what happens then I do not know, but there is an interchange of feasting between the two houses, and eventually the young man brings home his bride.

"It is interesting to notice that a sign of peace between two clans is the interchange of women by them. A woman is sent as an emissary of peace, and if she returned unharmed the clan is reckoned friendly by those who thus made overtures."

Another sketch by Rev. Barnhardt:—

"The young women were in their best; their bronze bodies shone after being specially washed and anointed with oil. They looked as fresh as new paint, speaking literally. Their heads were newly shaved, leaving ribs of woolly hair crossing from side to side. There were 150 of them gathered in the centre of a large space, all singing and dancing in unison with the male part of the assembly. These latter, to the number of 200 or 300, were dressed in most fantastic ways, paint and furs, feathers and hides, in every style.

A great Dance.
"Some had drums and wind instruments, others had spears and battle-axes. Some had belts formed of hundreds of cowrie shells, which jingled as they wriggled their bodies at a

tremendous velocity. Others had long fur boas, the tails of which, at certain intervals of the dance, they cast gently over the shoulder of the maiden of their choice, this attention being acknowledged by a graceful bow.

"Bright coloured European cloth was displayed with great pride. The band kept time and moved forward saluting the king, then retiring, gave place to the warriors, who, with uplifted weapons, made mimic warfare. So the rattle and noise increased till the dust rose in clouds. The missionary came in for his share of the salutations. After about an hour's performance the company broke up, only to continue their enjoyment in private houses. It was what the Americans call 'great.' One did not expect such excellence of display amongst natives. It did not take a great stretch of imagination to depict the scene after a successful raid into an enemy's country. It would be awful in its madness."

Yet another impression from Mr. Maxwell:—

"We have had some noisy neighbours lately. Some of the younger men have been doing honour to the memory of one of their number, singing over, and over and over, and over again, in a sort of song, '*O, yenga O, Sambo we a, a owe ya,*' or something that sounds like that (which is, I am told, a mixture of Jukun, Dinge, and Fulanchi), to the accompaniment of a drum and horn, especially the horn. It isn't so bad if they'd only play the drum, but when they get to snorting with that horn, it's kind of wearing when you

Songs in the Night.

want to sleep. If they'd only do it during the day, too, but they've done a good deal at night or in the early morning. However, '*komi risan dare, gari ya waye,*' as the Hausas say, ' However long the night, the day will break'; they've quit now, or almost so."

After one of our services, Mr. Guinter and I walked through the market and back round past the houses out into the farms and bush beyond. How true the lines are:—

> " The folk thereunder
> Bound, who should conquer,—slaves who should be kings;
> Hearing their one hope with an emp'y wonder,
> Sadly contented with a show of things."

Nemesis. Dark as their bodies are their minds, and darker still the souls of the sons and daughters of the Dark Continent. Weak, infant voices appeal to us stewards of the worship of the true God, of day and light and good out of the shadows of the midnight land. Unless we do our duty by them, unless we do our duty by these wards of ours, our modern European civilisation now penetrating Central Africa and our representatives of Greater Britain will find their nemesis in the cul-de-sac of Islam.

History of Missions in the Sudan

Treatment of New Converts, Church Discipline, Church Control, Polygamy:

> "Behold, a man of Ethiopia . . who said, 'What doth hinder me to be baptised?' And Philip said, 'If thou believest with all thine heart, thou mayest.' And he answered and said, 'I believe that Jesus Christ is the Son of God.'" *Acts viii. 27 and 36, 37.*

CHAPTER IX

AFRICA has always had a close connection with the history of the Jewish people, with Christ, and the early spread of Christianity. The north-east corner of it might almost be called the Place of Refuge. Abraham came to Egypt for food; Jacob and his sons went to Egypt to escape starvation; Christ as a baby was carried to Egypt to prevent His being slain in the Bethlehem massacres. The history of the life of Abraham is familiar to every child; his flight into Egypt is a landmark in his life. He, a Bedouin, and the son of a Bedouin, must have marvelled at the monuments of Egypt, the giant Pyramids and the mysterious Sphinx, we see before us to-day; the hoary sepulchres of the dawn of civilisation.

The name of Joseph is still well known in Egypt. Twelve years ago, on the summit of the Great Pyramid, a crowd of Arabs round me, I pointed out to them the land of Goshen, and told them of Yussif, the true servant of God. Had they ever heard of Yussif? **Yussif, the servant of God.**

"Had they not? Why, Yussif was the best-known man in Egypt. Why, yonder is the Yussif Canal, the Yussif monuments. Yussif! Why, everybody knows about Yussif."

The name of Alexander is unknown, though the second greatest city in Egypt, Alexandria, was founded by him. The names of the Ptolemys have gone from the memory of the Egyptians. The Roman conquest, Cleopatra has no meaning to them, but Joseph, Yussif lives in Egypt to-day.

Yonder, a little distance from Cairo city, stands the old Olive tree under which, tradition tells us, the Virgin Mother rested with her babe.

Africa gave an asylum to the infant Christ. Africa gave the Crossbearer to Christ, the Martyr and the Saviour.

While Europe, in that great tragedy, Europe that rules the world to-day, supplied the relentless, cynical, but cowardly judge; Asia, the stage, the scene, and the traitor; Africa came to the help of the Outcast, and bore His Cross. Shall not Africa be rewarded for this?

The first Missionary Institute. One of the first proselytes mentioned in the New Testament to whom the Gospel was preached, and who was baptised after the day of Pentecost, was once more an African. The first Foreign Missionary Institute for the training of men to go out as missionaries to the heathen world was established in Alexandria, in Egypt. It was in Egypt first that Christian men withdrew themselves to quiet meditation in the desert, founding the first monasteries.

The greatest library of antiquity was that in Alexandria, an eminently Christian library. It went up in flames during the conquest of North Africa by the armies of the false prophet.

The Coptic, Gyptic, Egyptian Churches date back to the first century after Christ.

In 1899 I discovered interesting monuments in the southern parts of the oasis of Charga in the neighbourhood of Beriis. An old Egyptian Temple had a propylon built on to it by the Romans with a Latin inscription. After the Roman came the Christian era, and the Pharaonic-Roman temple was turned into a Christian Cathedral. The heathen altar and the gods had been removed, and their places taken by the Table of the Lord. On both sides of this table were inscriptions on the wall drawn in red, remarkably well preserved; an inscription in Greek and an inscription in later Hieroglyphics, to the effect that this Temple had been consecrated to the service of Jehovah and Jesus by a bishop. It was dated early in the second century.

Then came the flood tide of Islam, and until 1840 Christianity had to exist in the Coptic monasteries of the desert, and in the underground cells, the cellar churches of Cairo.

About the middle of the nineteenth century modern missions commenced again in Egypt and North Africa.

The first two attempts emanated from the Church of England and the United Presbyterian

Modern Missions in Egypt.

Church of the United States. About the middle of the last century the C.M.S. commenced missionary operations in Cairo, and at the same time the United Presbyterian Church of America had its attention drawn to the distressing state in which the Coptic Church of Egypt had existed for centuries. But a few years later Bishop Gobat, the first Protestant Bishop of Jerusalem, who had sent missionaries to Abyssinia, attempted to build a line of stations from Jerusalem to Abyssinia, following the Nile. The history of this *Apostelstrasse,* as he named it, will be found in a future chapter of this book.

In 1865 the Church Missionary Society sent its missionaries up the Niger to Lokoja, the first border station of the Sudan regions. Other missions sprang up in North Africa, but the Sudan remained a closed land. Bishop Crowther made a journey up the Benué into the Central Sudan, but lost his boat and had to return. A few Roman Catholic missionaries in the Seventies of the last century, amongst them Brother Ohrwaldler, attempted mission work in the Eastern Sudan, and other French Roman Catholic missionaries penetrated into the Western Sudan from the Senegal, and reached Timbuktu.

Graham Wilmot Brooke.

Amongst the Protestants there was one lonely pioneer whose name was *Graham Wilmot Brooke,* on whose heart God had laid the Sudan, the waiting heart of Africa. He went up the Congo and the Ubangi until he stood on the north bend of that northern tributary of the Zaire (Congo).

MISSIONS IN THE SUDAN

He describes how he looked with longing eyes northward into the gloomy shadows of the great forests; how his mind traversed them, and reached the bush land of the ironstone plateau beyond, with its multitudes of tribes, its unexplored mountains and rivers. He saw strings of slaves go past his hut, driven southward into cannibal regions as food for the savages; he felt the agony, the pain, the sorrow of the heart of Africa. He stood at the gates of the Great Unknown, but the gates were closed, and he had to turn back.

A second time he attempted to reach the Central Sudan, and this time he went up the Niger, but while still a young man his health was undermined, his constitution broken, and with a prayer for the Sudan on his lips, he died at Lokoja, where he lies buried to-day. In the little cemetery just above the river where the Niger and the Benué meet, he lies there keeping watch at the gateway of the Central Sudan.

About the same time, Dr. H. Grattan Guinness was considerably exercised in mind over the letters that had come home from Wilmot Brooke, and at a meeting of Y.M.C.A. secretaries in the middle-west of the United States, he spoke of the sorrows of the Sudan, and fifty of the secretaries rose to band themselves together for the evangelisation of the greatest unevangelised field of the world, the Sudan. A party of them went to the west coast of Africa, and attempted to form a line of stations towards Timbuktu. But the Guinea Coast, the white man's grave, took a heavy toll of

Dr. H. Grattan Guinness.

their lives. Again and again men went out. The Mission is still in existence, but they have not been able to get very far inland.

Central Sudan Mission.
A little later, Mr. Hermann Harris, Mr. Rendell Harris, and a number of other good Christian men in England attempted to reach the Central Sudan by way of Tripoli and the Sahara. Mr. H. Harris, with about fifteen young men, went to Tripoli to study the Hausa language, but the Turkish Moslem rule made a traverse of the Sahara impossible, and most of the men returned. Two of them went round the west coast of Africa and into the Niger Territories. One fell ill and had to go home, and the other was slain and eaten by cannibals in the Bauchi Hill Country.

Yet another attempt to reach the Central Sudan was made from Toronto by Mr. Bingham, who, with two companions, went to Lagos. One of them succeeded in reaching Northern Nigeria, but died there. Mr. Bingham, who acted for a time as Bishop Hill's secretary, almost died in Africa of fever, and returned later to Canada. Bishop Hill, whose name has just been mentioned, went out with a number of C.M.S. missionaries, eight in all, to the Niger Territories in 1893. All succumbed within a year and a half, with the exception of one.

Toll for the brave! the brave that dared and died! Would that Sudan ever be reached?

In 1898 began the modern conquest of these lands left alone for so long.

A short history of the Eastern Sudan may not

MISSIONS IN THE SUDAN

be out of place here in order that we may the better understand the problems and prospects of modern missionary work in those far-off regions.

"The Ethiopia of the ancients is the Sudan of to-day, with Abyssinia and Erythrea included; it stretched from Thebes in Egypt to the countries inhabited by savages south of the junction of the Blue and White Niles, but how far south cannot be ascertained. The ancient kings of the Sudan several times conquered Upper Egypt, and consequently we find sculptured figures and hieroglyphics after the manner of the old Egyptian ones on certain ancient monuments in the Sudan, but with meanings of their own which so far have proved a sealed book. The city of Meroe appears to have been the ancient capital. Here the famous Meroe pyramids are to be seen, different in shape from any in Egypt, the base being about three times its height, which also is lower than any of the Egyptian ones, and only some 30 to 40 feet.

"Professor Petrie is credited with saying that Meroe was most probably the home of the great Queen of Sheba, and that her famous expedition to Solomon took place from here. Certain it is that there was a succession of great queens known as Candace, and the portraits of these are to be seen on the monuments to this day, and formidable looking ladies they must have been, if their portraits in stone are to be believed. They are pictured as being extremely stout, grasping a crowd of prisoners by their hair in one hand, and

Queen Candace.

holding a battle-axe in the other. A condition of civilisation existed many hundreds of years B.C. which did not exist in the country ten years ago. There is the great past, and the very modern present, marked in stone and other work, but of the handiwork of the countless generations that have passed between there is nothing but a blank.

"The site of Meroe is on the east bank of the Nile, between the fifth and sixth cataracts, about half a mile from the river. Between the two cataracts there is a long stretch of navigable river connected with the land routes leading to the Atbara and the Blue Nile. Thus the ancient city occupied a position of strategic importance, and in the seventh century B.C., was all-powerful, but was destroyed at the end of the fourth century by the Kings of Axum.

"The excavations here carried out by Professor Garstang have settled once for all the site of Meroe. They have also settled the site of the temple of Amon, where the Kings of Ethiopia were crowned.

Table of the Sun.
"Readers of Herodotus will remember that he speaks of a Table of the Sun in a green meadow outside the city of Meroe. Many interesting remains have been unearthed, among them the emblem of the cult, a large solar disc, was found amid the ruins of the western wall. Several panels of Merotic writing tablets of the Lion-God and the King have been brought home.

"Part of the Metropolis has been excavated, and many interesting relics discovered. One of them, taken from behind the high altar of the Temple of Amon, is part of a human skeleton, and at the bottom of the chamber a place for a sarcophagus had evidently been prepared and walled with brick. 'From that,' says Professor Garstang, 'it is possible, considering the position and circumstances of the discovery, that the burial indicates a human sacrifice (the representative of Amon himself) at the dedication of the Temple.'"

The Eastern Sudan was a Christian country before it became Mohammedan. Christianity appears to have been introduced through Abyssinia, it is said by St. Athanasius, but how far this can be relied on is uncertain. The remains of Christian Churches are to be seen to this day at Soha, ten miles south of Khartum, on the Blue Nile, and in various places in the Dongola province. The invasion of Ethiopia by the Arabs from Arabia, about 700 A.D., brought the Moslem creed into the country, and all Christian Churches and monuments were speedily razed to the ground. *Early Christianity.*

To recapitulate here the occupation of the States of the Sudan by the European Powers—Great Britain, France, Germany—within the last twelve years is unnecessary. As a result of the occupation, as stated repeatedly in this book, an advance of Mohammedanism became possible amongst the warlike pagan tribes in the South. And this aroused some of our leading Christian men to take an interest in the fate of the tribes. *Modern Missions.*

To-day our missionary enterprise in the Sudan is carried on by five Protestant missionary societies at the following stations.

In the Eastern Sudan, the Church Missionary Society—if we take Khartum, Khartum North, and Omdurman as one centre—has two posts (*a*) Khartum, (*b*) Bor.

The United Presbyterians of America also have two stations in the Eastern Sudan, (*a*) Khartum, (*b*) Doleib Hill. There is no Protestant mission station west of the Nile, between the Nile and the Niger territories. In Northern Nigeria, the C.M.S. has seven mission stations—Lokoja, Bida, Katsa, Zaria, Kuta, Panyam, and Kabir—besides one or two out-stations.

The Sudan Interior Mission, a result of Mr. Bingham's former journey to Africa, has five stations : Patagi, Wushishi, Egbe, Kpada, and Paiko.

The fourth missionary society is that of the Menonite Brethren in Christ. Their leader is Mr. Banfield, and they have two stations : a station at Shonga, and another one at Jebba.

The Sudan United Mission. Fifthly, the Sudan United Mission, with seven stations ; Rumasha, Bukuru, Langtang, Ibi, Wukari, Donga. and M'bula, and two out-stations at present unoccupied. This gives to the Sudan altogether twenty-five mission stations, with less than half-a-dozen out-stations in a country larger than the whole of Europe, minus Russia. If the Pagan tribes are to be evangelised in the Sudan they must be evangelised by native agents, and it would, therefore, appear advisable that the energy of the very few European missionaries at present in that country should be directed towards the teaching and training of natives.

There are certain principles that it is well to bear in mind. These principles have been gathered on visits to various parts of Africa, and result from a study of the methods of some twenty-five missionary societies at work in that continent, and should, therefore, be of interest and value.

To begin with, we must bear in mind that the African races are baby races, and that converts from these races to Christianity are children and not full-grown men. To begin with, they have not at their disposal the inherited character built up by some thirty or forty generations of Christian forefathers; and, secondly, as compared with the people in the East, they are only in the initial stages of civilisation. Reading and writing, geography and scientific knowledge are to them unknown accomplishments, though many among the Chinese, Japanese, or Indians have them already at their disposal. The African may be physically the most developed; mentally and spiritually he is only a child before and after he professes conversion.

Methods must, therefore, be adopted with them different from the methods in use in the East. The trust the native African reposes in his spiritual White Father, the trust of the child in the parent, must be carefully guarded, as it is a lever of considerable influence for good. If the

Methods of Work.

missionary in the East needs to be careful in his life before the native converts, the missionary in the South needs to be more so. *Pranks* should never be played on native converts, and what is known as *larking* is disastrous.

But that does not mean that games, such as football, cricket, paper-chase, or others should be avoided. On the contrary, these are the very things that bring missionaries and converts more closely together. The best father is a companion to his son, and, as far as possible, a playmate. The successful missionary in Africa finds himself very much more *in loco parentis* to his converts than the missionary in the East.

I hardly know how many times I have pointed out the great virtue for Africa—patience. It is in the possession of a superabundance of it that the strength of our Christian religious emissary in Africa lies.

Because a child makes incorrect statements, or is even found to tell untruths, the child does not cease to be the child of the father. Because a child has appropriated certain tempting sweets, cakes or bits of sugar, it is not driven from the home and thrown out into the streets. Faults must be corrected; sin placed into such relative perspective that the native convert realises it is sin without its being pointed out to him continually by the missionary. The best educated child has not been brought up with a multitude of "Don'ts." If a baby is about to place a poisonous berry into its mouth, "Don't" is a poor preventative. Offer it a handful of strawberries, and the poisonous berry will drop.

Missionaries will do well to praise the converts for all their good points, and to hold up before them healthy, manly Christian ideals. The best missionary has a vast storehouse of parables and stories, just as the best parent is overflowing with tales for his boys. Should a convert be found appropriating things that do not belong to him, that is to say, if he steals and knows that he is stealing—for many things that appear to us Europeans as theft are to the natives thoughtless appropriation of things that he deems common property—but if a boy steals and knows that he has done wrong, he should be punished for it. And the best punishment is the moral punishment. *A Storehouse of Parables.*

Here is an example from my last year's trans-African expedition. A young carrier, Audu Gajere (the little David), had been appointed to assist Peter in tent duties. There was an abundance of food for every man in camp, meat and guinea corn; but I was running short of bread and flour. Almost the last batch of bread had been baked. There were only four small loaves left, and two or three pounds of flour. I had been out in the bush trying to secure meat for the men; had succeeded, and tired out, sat down to my evening meal. There was only half a small loaf lying by the plate. *Stealing Bread.*

"Peter, bring me a loaf of bread."

Peter went into the tent. Peter came back.

"Please sir, the bread is finished."

"But, Peter, there were four loaves this morning. I happened to look into the box when I took one loaf with me hunting."

"No, sir, the bread is finished."

"But, Peter, where has it gone?"

"I do not know, sir."

"Who was in charge of the tent?" (As there were instruments and valuable collections stored away in the tent, a sentinel was always kept posted in front).

"Who was in charge of the tent?"

"Musa" (Moses).

"Call Musa."

Musa appeared.

"Yes, sir."

Musa and the loaves. "Musa, I had four loaves of bread in the tent this morning. They have gone. You have been in charge of the tent. Where have they gone to? It is not that I am anxious about the bread, but I dislike to have untrustworthy men in my caravan. Where is the bread?"

"I do not know, sir."

"Musa, you were in charge of the tent. The bread has been taken out of the tent. You will go without food until you tell me where it has gone."

A stolid "Yes, sir!" and the boys depart. Musa was a man of about forty-five years of age, older than the white man in years, but in mind and soul a child.

Next day Musa had to do without food.

Towards the evening a dejected-looking, very self-conscious man, he came to the tent.

"Please, sir, may I speak to you?"

"Yes, Musa, what is it?"

"Please, sir, I do not like to tell tales against my fellow-workmen."

"No, Musa, I respect you for it. But, you see, to live peaceably together we must be able to trust one another. Who took the bread?"

Musa in a dilemma.

"Please, sir, must I tell you?"

"Yes, Musa, I must ask you to speak. Come, now, who stole it?"

"Audu Gajere, sir. He went to the tent, as he is a personal boy, and I let him go in. When he came out I saw his jacket bulging out in front, and I am sure he has taken the loaves."

"Thank you, Musa."

And calling towards the camping-ground of the men, I instructed the headman to give Musa his portion of food.

Next I called my head boy, Dangana. Dangana came.

"Dan, you have heard from Peter that somebody has taken three loaves of bread, and there is only this half loaf left. Call Audu Gajere."

Audu Gajere came.

"Audu Gajere, you have taken three loaves of bread out of the tin in my tent yesterday, have you not?"

"No, sir."

"Audu Gajere, speak the truth. You have taken those loaves."

"No, sir."

Poor Audu Gajere.

"Dangana, Audu Gajere is a thief and a stranger to the truth. He must have been very hungry to steal his master's bread. I wonder whether he is hungry now. Give him that half loaf of bread, and tell him to eat it."

Dan picked up the loaf, and wanted to put it into the hands of Audu Gajere. But Audu Gajere stood with his hands stiff down by his side. Then came the following conversation between the two boys:

Dan: "Audu Gajere, our master says you are to take this bread and eat it."

No answer.

Dan: "Audu Gajere, will you take it, and take it quickly?"

No answer.

Then Dan did something which he had not ventured to do before. He raised his voice in my presence.

"Au—du—Ga—je—re—!"

He took Audu Gajere's hand; he opened it, put the loaf into it, turned him round, and marched him off to the kitchen camp fire. By the time the half loaf was in Audu Gajere's hand, tears were streaming down his face.

Next day, Dan had to make bread of the last tin of flour. The evening came.

"Dan, bring me Audu Gajere."

Audu Gajere was brought. The two hundred people in camp had become attentive, and were watching silently.

"Give Audu Gajere a loaf of my bread. These are the last three loaves, and if he likes it so much he may have it, and I will do without it."

"Please, sir, I don't want to take it."

"Yes, Audu Gajere, you must. You see, unless I can trust my boys as they can trust me, we cannot live happily together; and I cannot send you away here in the bush, so I must punish you. You take this loaf of bread and eat it."

Sobbing and crying, Audu Gajere withdrew with his loaf of bread. The next evening the same exhibition, and the third evening saw it repeated. By that time little David had gone all to pieces. He cried all the afternoon, and when he was called up he just threw himself down, and sobbed most bitterly.

Audu Gajere's Sorrow.

"Audu Gajere, you have never told me yet, did you take those three loaves of bread out of the tent?"

"Yes, sir, I did. I was a thief. I told the untruth. But I will never, never, never, never do it again."

And he never, never, never, never did.

From the treatment of personal boys and the treatment of converts to Church discipline is but one step. And what holds good for the one holds good for the other. Don't condone wrong, but be careful about the method of punishment. As long as converts are despised by their own people they are usually spiritually healthy; but when Christianity becomes fashionable amongst the tribes, the time of danger begins. And the fundamental principles of Christianity are apt to become lax. This is leprosy, and leads to death after a frightfully painful period of disease, when limb after limb drops and moulders into the grave, until the whole is dead.

Church Government. Church Government in Africa should be in the hands of the missionaries for many years to come; but as the children grow up, slowly, responsibility according to their strength may be placed upon their shoulders.

A serious problem which all our new African Churches have to face is the problem of polygamy. Missionary societies working on the Congo, on the Zambesi, in West Africa, and South Africa have not been able to see eye to eye in this. Some hold that no heathen can be baptised as long as he has several wives. Others hold that a man may be baptised but not allowed to the Communion Table as long as he indulges in polygamy. And others again maintain that a heathen convert cannot be recognised as an evangelist or teacher until he has but one wife.

Amongst the lower types of pagans, Dr. Ratzel, a friend of mine and late Professor of Geography of the University of Leipzig, says polygamy, with its attendant evils would appear to exercise the determining influence in respect of morality. The unclothed tribe is essentially a primitive one, and being poor, cannot acquire wives by purchase.

And Dr. Silva White says: "Although polygamy, as an institution is almost universal in

Africa, it is only the more advanced tribes which possess the capital to indulge in any excess. Polygamy gives rise to the slave trade, and a herd of other evils."

There are a considerable number of tribes in the Sudan that are monogamists, and for them the problem question of polygamy amongst converts does not exist. Let us face that whole question as in everything else, remembering the two sides to it. The Congo Missions especially lay weight on this, that once a man has married several wives, he is responsible for them, and to send them back to the families whence they came is, in some cases, impossible. Shall he turn his wives into the streets and make them public women? Surely the remedy would be worse than the disease. In this, of course, all agree, that no man can hold office in a church who is not the husband of one wife, according to the Scriptures; and also, if a convert after conversion marries more than one wife, Church discipline should step in, and he should be put out of bounds. The African Church will, for many years to come, be best administered on the patriarchal or episcopalean system. While in the British Empire the Dominions govern themselves through parliaments, the administration of the Central African Colonies is autocratic. And as the Sudanese people, mentally and spiritually, are to-day but children, the principles that rule the political administration there should rule the Church government also.

Polygamy.

The Success or Otherwise of Missions in Central Africa

Proverbs such as the following by Booker Washington are worth remembering:—

1. All forms of labour are dignified, and all forms of idleness a disgrace.
2. No man who has the privilege of rendering service to his fellows ever makes a sacrifice.
3. It is a difficult thing to make a good Christian out of a hungry man.
4. I will learn to love all people, and it is along the road of love and service that my race will make progress.

CHAPTER X

THE beginnings of missionary enterprise in Africa lie in the West and the South of the continent. The vanguard of the preachers of Christ in Africa lies buried on the Slave Coast in the Gulf of Guinea. Endless fightings between white settlers and natives in South Africa proved as great a hindrance to the success of missionary work there as the climatic conditions were on the Guinea Coast.

Four pairs of path-finders laid the foundations for the success of Christian teaching in Africa of to-day. These were Moffat and Livingstone for South Africa; Krapf and Rebman for East Africa; Koelle and Schoen for West Africa; and Bishop Gobat and Dr. Pfaender for the Moslem parts of North Africa. While the latter two never worked as missionaries in North Africa, yet their writings, and those whom they sent, formed the basis for our modern missionary propaganda.

Missionary Path-finders.

To speak of Livingstone and Moffat there is no need. Their monuments are to-day in Lovedale, Livingstonia, Barotsi Land, Nyassaland, Garanganze, and Banza-Manteke.

How do we get from Moffat to Banza-Manteke? Surely it is a far cry from one to the other; yet there is a perfectly simple line of events, following one another.

Livingstone married Moffat's daughter. Stanley found Livingstone. The Livingstone Inland Mission resulted from Stanley's opening the Congo, and Banza-Manteke realised the most remarkable Pentecostal blessing on the Congo.

Krapf and Rebman, the second pair of pioneers, first told of the great Lake regions of Tanganyika and Ukerewe. When Krapf buried his wife at Mombasa, he wrote home to the Church Missionary Society, " I have put the first corn of seed into the ground. It will bring forth a rich harvest." The harvest we have to-day in Uganda.

Three years ago, in 1907, I visited Mengo, the capital of Uganda. When crossing Lake Victoria I wrote :

Uganda. Away to the south stretches the vast level of the greatest African lake, the Ukerewe, as the natives call it, or the Victoria Nyanza, as the explorers named it. A lazy warm breeze just ruffles the surface, as our magnificent modern steamer ploughs her way through the water. Here and there small rocky islands, covered with green shrubs, arise out of the unclear yellow deep. Five or six hours' sailing, and the water becomes clearer and takes a green tint. As we leave Port Florence Bay the lake looks quite innocent, though one is told that at times tropical thunderstorms lash its face into towering waves. This great

Central African lake is as large as Holland and Denmark combined.

Within a few days the well-built railroad has carried us from Mombasa on the coast through some of the most beautiful scenery in the world, right into the heart of Central Africa. Through the fever land and open plain, with its thousands and thousands of antelopes, gazelles, zebras, giraffes, and many other kinds of wild game, the train has sped its way—past Kilimanjaro and Mount Kenia—we have hastened onward up the escarpment and wended our way through the rift-valley, and now we have arrived at the famous headwaters of the Nile. Beyond the horizon lies the Ruwenzori, the highest mountain range in Africa, with its snow-clad peaks and lonely glaciers, sending the thawed ice into Lake Albert.

What did we come to see? The beauties, the exceeding beauties of nature? The magnificent engineering feat of that East African railroad? (that white elephant, which in spite of people's prophecies, is already paying its dividends). Did we come to see the solved riddle of the sources of the Nile? the Caput Nili? or perchance the Mountains of the Moon? No; a greater and more wonderful sight. We have come to see the miracle of modern Missions, a mighty heathen nation, brought out of slavery and midnight darkness, out of superstition and savagery, into the light and liberty of the faith of Christ.

On approaching Entebbe, we sighted a curious

building crowning a hill on the horizon, a building with three conically-shaped towers.

"What is that remarkable structure?" we asked the captain.

<small>The Light=
house of
Uganda.</small>
"That is the lighthouse of Uganda," came the smiling reply; "the Cathedral of Bishop Tucker."

On my visit the next day I was led by the Bishop to the great House of God. I was told the building had been erected by the natives themselves, members of the chief's family bringing wood and water, mortar and stones to build the House of God. On approaching one of the side doors of the Cathedral it was found that the doors were locked. I enquired from the Bishop why the doors of the Cathedral were not left open so that people might go inside, and in the silence and shadow meditate and pray.

Said the Bishop, "Our difficulty is to get the Cathedral empty so that it may be cleaned out. If we left the doors open the place would never be empty."

The difficulty in Uganda to-day is not to get people to church but to keep them out of church. Christianity is fashionable there to-day. A Christian is not a foreign devil, an infidel, a son of a dog, but a Christian in Uganda is the respectable gentleman, and Moslems and pagans are looked down upon from a superior height. Multitudes desire to be baptised, and the problem in Uganda to-day is to keep out those who may not live up to their profession.

I have just been informed that the Uganda

Cathedral has been burned down, but there is little doubt that a larger and more imposing structure will take its place.

The third West African pair of missionaries, are Koelle and Schoen, both of them philologists, who, by gathering vocabularies, beginning Scripture translations, and securing a considerable amount of information as to the tribal relationships of the Niger Territories, paved the way for our missionary advance. Dr. Koelle's "Polyglotta Africana" was written more than fifty years ago, and has been to this day the basis of comparative philological studies. His Hausa Dictionary and Hausa translations, and translation of parts of the Scriptures, while faulty in many respects, were remarkable books if one remembers the material that was at that time at his disposal.

"Polyglotta Africana."

Dr. Schoen went further afield than Dr. Koelle, and studied the languages on the shore of Lake Chad, compiling a Kanuri Grammar, and gathering Kanuri proverbs and stories. Bishop Crowther and the late Wilmot Brooke followed in the footsteps of Koelle and Schoen.

The coast region has seen the beginnings of a harvest in Yoruba land, but further inland in Northern Nigeria, and even more in the French Western Sudan, Christian missionary work is in most important districts conspicuous by its absence.

The fourth and last pair of early missionary enthusiasts were Bishop Gobat and Dr. Pfaender for the lands of North Africa. Bishop Gobat had

"Apostel-strasse."

been interested for a long time in Abyssinia, and he, as the first Protestant Anglican Bishop of Jerusalem, built the "Apostelstrasse," a line of stations named after the twelve apostles from Alexandria to Abyssinia. They included the following:—Alexandria, Cairo, Assiut, Luxor, Assuan, Wady-Halfa, Dongola, Berber, Khartum, and Benishongul. But Bishop Gobat was before his time. The Apostelstrasse was deserted, and only the two stations of Alexandria and Cairo were maintained. The two German hospitals, the two schools and the two churches in these cities are the last remnants of the Apostelstrasse.

The C.M.S. work, the American Presbyterian mission, the North Africa Mission, the Egypt General Mission, the Dutch Mission, and the Sudan Pioneer Mission are later and most of them indirectly the outgrowths of Bishop Gobat's prayers and plans. Dr. Pfaender in his Mizan-ul-Hacque (the Balance of Truth) gave to missionaries to the Moslems a weapon of offence and defence of excellently-tempered steel. His writings of fifty years ago can to-day hardly be improved upon.

The Balance of Truth.

Now, as to the comparative success of missionary enterprise in Africa, and the whys and the wherefores of such success. A cursory glance will immediately show that in North Africa nearest to Europe we have the least success. In South Africa, where tribes have been under European control for many decades, our success is not over brilliant. But in Central

Africa, the last acquired, the last reached, the least touched by Europeans, with a comparatively small staff of missionaries, we find magnificent success. There were missionaries in Egypt fifty years ago when no white man had ever seen Uganda. To-day Uganda is Christian, but in Egypt we have a Mohammedan State, and from the nine millions of Moslems the converts to Christianity cannot be counted by hundreds. This is not the fault of our most devoted missionaries there. Was there ever a greater missionary enthusiast of modern days than Thornton, of Cairo? The educational and evangelistic work of the American Presbyterians, of the C.M.S., the North Africa Mission, the Egypt General Mission, and others is splendid. The organisations are in perfect working order, the men are well-chosen, but the Moslem fanaticism makes work difficult. *Islam in North Africa.*

And what we find in Egypt we find in the other States of North Africa, only Egypt has a greater chance than Tripoli, Tunis, Algiers, or Morocco to find its way to Christ, for it has more missionaries in proportion, and is under British control. Christian religious emissaries to North Africa should be choice men of deep spiritual devotion, marked intellectuality, and considerable adaptability. Thank God for the devoted spiritual crusaders in North Africa. Would that their numbers were multiplied. Would that their overwhelming difficulties were more adequately understood.

South Africa presents a very different problem. It is, in this case, not the fanaticism of an anti-Christian religion that creates difficulties. In South Africa we have the vagaries, the aberrations of the Christian faith developing dangers. We are dealing, in this case, with dangers, with combinations of spiritual dynamite; the race hatred between Britain and Boer, between white and black, the lack of help vouchsafed by Government men and settlers to native training institutions, such as Lovedale and others, the new anti-white movement of the Ethiopian Church; such conflicting currents rising and falling periodically, and converging in various combinations, show that the religious atmosphere of South Africa is heavily charged with powerful, ethical problems. The unification of South Africa under a union control is a step in the right direction. It is also believed by men who know South Africa well that the Ethiopian movement has attained its fullest development. The enthusiasm for foreign missions which I found in the Dutch Reformed Church in South Africa a few years ago, promises a great future for this Church both in South Africa and Central Africa. Neither North Africa nor South Africa, as far as results go, can for a moment be compared with the success which missions have had among the Pagan tribes of Central Africa.

The Ethiopian Church.

There are four outstanding fields, Uganda, Livingstonia-Nyassaland, Banza-Manteke, and Yoruba Land. Two of these most successful mission fields belong to the Church Missionary Society, one to the Presbyterians, and one to the Baptists. In these four districts Christianity prevails to-day. The two thousand native evangelists, ministers, and missionaries supported by the Church of Uganda, the eighty thousand school children in the Presbyterian Schools of British Central Africa, the self-sacrificing devotion of the Christians on the Congo, and the religious enthusiasm displayed by many of the Yorubas, are tokens that we are justified in our expectation that God means the Pagan tribes of Central Africa to be won for the faith of Christ.

In lands where the missionaries have neither to battle against the uncompromising fanaticism of another faith, nor the lowered prestige of Europeans such as we find in certain parts on the Gold Coast, nor against the race hatred so long, alas, exhibited in South Africa, we may look for the greatest success in our missionary enterprise ; and the experience of the last thirty years bears witness that we have reason for our expectations. *Where to expect the greatest success.*

The lessons the Christian Church has had to learn in the time of Bishop Crowther and Wilmot Brooke in West Africa have been learned.

We must on no account allow into the Church those who have not been adequately tested as to their Christian character, truthfulness, honesty and morality. The lion-faced leader of the Church of Uganda is laying himself out to have his Central African Church live out the experience gained in the West.

Child Nations.

The first principle of successful missionary enterprise in Central Africa is that a Christian character must be built up amongst the child nations through the formation of Christian habits, and that can only be done through an adequate Christian school system. Where, therefore, in Central Africa we have the best schools, we find the greatest success in the mission. If we limit our energies amongst these child people to evangelising, we shall be doing in Africa what we would surely never agree to for our children in the homeland. Evangelistic meetings assisted by evening classes for the grown-up, and regular school training assisted by evangelistic meetings for the children, are the ideal methods.

The following is a plan of an educational system adopted by the Sudan United Mission, to be worked out in Northern Nigeria. A similar system has for some time been in working order in Uganda and British Central Africa.

I. Elementary Education.
   (a) Village Schools (at every Mission Station personal and village boys are taught to read and write).
   (b) Freed Slaves' Home. (170 boys and girls are mentally and industrially trained at Rumasha).
   (c) A school for the sons of Chiefs on the lines of the Princes' School at Uganda.

II. Secondary Education.
   (a) Seminary for the training of teachers.
   (b) Technical Institution.
      (1) Handicrafts.
      (2) Agricultural or horticultural.

MISSIONS IN CENTRAL AFRICA

III. The former Institutions should lead in time to the establishment of a rudimentary University at which the following four faculties should be represented:—

    (1) Science.
    (2) Arts.
    (3) Medicine.
    (4) Theology.

It is hardly more than a hundred years since the first missionaries went to Africa. Fifty years ago Livingstone broke a way into the interior of that continent, and to-day there are hardly a hundred miles square of its inhabited territories unexplored. When a little over a hundred years ago, Mungo Park, as the first explorer of the interior of Africa, visited Timbuktu, and on his second tour lost his life half way down the Niger in the Bussa Rapids, the lands lying to the east of him were utterly unknown. People had heard about Chadda, but whether Chadda was the Upper Nile flowing south of the Sahara parallel with it, or whether it was a great lake or a new river was entirely problematic. Some held one opinion, some the other. The Congo basin was one vast "*terra incognita,*" the Kalahari Desert, the "ultima Thule" that had ever been reached by members of the Dutch East India Company in Cape Colony. Mozambique was a European trade centre, but further north the land lay beyond the reach of Europeans.

[margin: Terra Incognita.]

In the volumes written about Africa since the days of Strabo, Eratosthenes, Ptolemy, Pliny, Eusebius, Pausanias, and the more modern Leo Africanus, and Mohammed el Tounsy in the Middle Ages, and then during the flood tide of explorers and writers of the last century, there has always been something new from Africa. "*Quid novo ex Africa*," had become proverbial. And missionaries had a very large share in bringing geographical light into the Dark Continent.

"Quid novo ex Africa."

Men who had a special share in this and did good geographical work were Moffat, Krapf, Rebman, Livingstone, Arnot, and many others. And some of the sons of these missionary pathfinders are at the present day administrators in our African Colonies.

The fifteen hundred missionaries working in Africa are far less compared to the population than we find in the Far East, and, according to the extent of country, they are utterly disproportionate.

Fifteen Hundred Missionaries.

Comparisons are odious, and yet consciously and unconsciously we are comparing causes and effects, men and means, subjects and objects in life; and it is oftentimes nothing but prudery that prevents us from giving an expression to our views. In warfare he would be counted an inefficient officer who would either understate or overstate the men or means at his disposal in his report.

With the new "Union" in South Africa accomplished, a union of our Protestant missionary enterprise there seems desirable, and would probably set free a few of the workers for the more needed posts in the interior. East Africa needs all it has, West Africa needs all it has, and North Africa needs more, but large tracts of Central Africa are at the present day a "No Man's Land" from the religious standpoint.

While in the East, amongst the ancient nations of the Mongol races, and in India, evangelists and university professors are the types of men wanted, Africa needs teachers, teachers of character, manly pedagogues, men with sound training, spiritually, mentally, and physically. The most successful missionaries in Africa will be men of the type of Mackay, the engineer; Livingstone, the doctor; Wilmot Brooke, the young Army officer. The winning of the tribe of Africa does not demand men of vast strategic attainments, generals, or admirals; nor does it need superlative culture. It needs just a considerable number of straight Captains and B.A.'s of our Universities; captains of cricket elevens, captains of football teams, successful engineers, and industrious farmers; a number of strong, keen, manly men. This type of men imbued with the enthusiasm for Christian missionary enterprise, will meet the needs of the Africa of to-day. But above and beyond all, that which is needed in every part of the foreign field is truth. Hypocrites may be able to exist in the Church at home, but hypocrites and shams will be found out soon enough by the natives of

Types of Men needed.

O

Central Africa, and success will not crown their labours.

Livingstone was a strong man and true, and his natives loved him. Mackay was true; he lived up to his profession. That was why the young men of Mengo were ready to go to the death for the faith they had taken from the lips of Mackay. Richardson of Banza-Manteke saw the great revival on the Congo, when, regardless of consequences, he attempted to live up to the injunctions of the Christ as revealed in the New Testament. We may hide our thoughts through many words from men, but we shall not permanently deceive the questioning eyes of children. The ease with which it appears to be possible to deceive trustful infants for awhile may be made use of, but sooner or later the child will penetrate the disguise and tear away the subterfuges of deceit, and we shall never have its confidence again.

What is needed to-day in Africa is true Christian religion. God give it to that land of children and slaves.

Rice Christians.
The last and most important point in the policy of missionary enterprise in Africa, a point that is frequently lost sight of, is the danger of denationalisation, and of bringing up what is known in China as "rice Christians," people who profess Christianity because of the advantages accruing to them from such profession, or people who become strangers to their own tribe by "monkeying" the white man. It is, of course, not only the missionary

who, at times, has made a mistake in his strong desire to win the people for Christ, but more than the missionary, the trader, and Government man has by introducing the veneer of European languages, of European clothing, and European vices, taken more than his share in weakening tribal strength and stamina in some cases, and in others in separating and estranging those natives he has gathered round him as his servants, employees, or troops, from their own people. The idea is wrong in principle that the Central African can be developed on European lines. Unconsciously we shall be making the mistake in Central Africa that has been made in the United States when the slaves were liberated. The negroes are not a full-grown nation; they are children, and as children they must be treated.

The first principle of Christianisation and administration in Central Africa should be that all missionaries and Government men teaching and administering should acquire the most important native language in use by the people amongst whom they labour.

Secondly, where the natives wear clothes, such as in Northern Nigeria or Uganda, European dress should not be introduced among them, and their imitating white men in appearance should be deprecated. Rather than introduce European handicrafts, the rudimentary native artisan should be trained; his cast-iron tools, changed into steel stools; his simple weaving apparatus be developed into a larger time-saving hand-loom.

Methods of Teaching.

Many of the negroes, as already stated, are splendid mechanics, and suddenly to introduce European methods of sowing or harvesting would not be helpful. A considerable number of ploughs have been sent out to Central Africa only to rust there. The first condition for using a plough in Central Africa is to improve the breed of horses and oxen, and to do away with the Tetse-fly in the river valleys. To think that we can train the Central African in English and educate him in English is folly. The Moslem, in advancing his religion, learns the native language and spreads his faith in that language, though he is considerably handicapped by having to use Arabic for his prayers, and the Koran, which is not allowed to be translated, in the original language of Mohammed. The Christian religion has no such handicap, and is, on that ground, more adapted and more adaptable to Central African conditions.

The thought that if school boys in Africa learn English a vast amount of reading matter and literature will be open to them is perfectly correct. But it is also correct that about half the reading matter thus given to them would be objectionable and harmful. Furthermore, the English tongue will probably never absolutely dominate Africa.

To produce English such as the following (a specimen from India), is nothing to be proud of. "*And we bewholed the hole phermament of heavens and stars and the school sticking reflected upside down in the pond errected by our worthy Collector.*" We smile at this English, and well we may, but there is contained in it an underlying lesson we had better learn. If English forms the basis of education in the Mission field, the purposes for which the school has been established will be " reflected upside down." We shall attain the opposite of what we are aiming at.

" Reflected upside down."

There are several most virile languages in Africa. It is for us to give to the young people a carefully-selected list of books in their own languages, and thus gradually train up Christian civilised African tribes to occupy a responsible and respected position in the council of the nations, the parliament of mankind.

Missionary Politics; True Christian Imperialism

O grant us minds like Thine
  That compassed all the nations,
That swept o'er land and sea and loved the
    least of all;
  Great things attempting for the Lord,
  Expecting mighty things from God.

CHAPTER XI

"SHUF HUNAK" (Look there), said the young chief of the Bongo tribe, as he sat on a mat at my feet.

The wild uninhabited wilderness lay behind us. We had entered the Gazelle River province (Bahr-el-Ghazal), and when we approached the district of the Bongo people my tired carriers received a very remarkable welcome from the inhabitants. Led by their chief, they came to meet us, singing and shouting like a crowd of children; they ran along by the side of my carriers, relieving them of their loads and rendering glad and useful service. The largest hamlet of the tribe had been reached, and we were encamped on an open piece of ground near it. The tent had been pitched and the camp fires were alight.

"Shuf hunak" (Look there), said the strong, dusky young prince, as, after luncheon in the early afternoon, I sat in my deck chair in the grateful shade of a shea tree. Pointing to a little village a short distance away,

"Look there! Do you see those large houses in the centre of the village?"

"Yes, what of them?"

"They are the houses of Mohammedan traders, our old enemies."

"Enemies?" I questioned. "Why your enemies? You speak their language—Arabic."

"Yes," the chief answered, "I understand their language, but I hate them."

"Why should you hate them?"

"Hate them!" he repeated. "I hate them like poison, Aulad-es-shaitan" (Children of the devil).

"I hate them!"

And then he proceeded to relate to me the history of his people, which I will endeavour to reproduce in as few words as may be.

Once upon a time.

"Once upon a time my people were the most powerful in all this country. The Bongos ruled north, south, east and west of the great Sudd swamp. They were, as you can see in us few remnants, powerful, bold, and warlike. At that time the Mohammedan Arabs came from the north country and took Khartum. They advanced farther south, and tried to make slaves of my fore-fathers. But my fore-fathers fought them with varying success.

"Never were my people slaves. But war, year in, year out, told upon our number. From a powerful nation we dwindled down until we became a small tribe of only ten thousand fighting men. More than twenty years ago, when my father was chief of the tribe, a great Moslem army came from Omdurman. They entered our country unexpectedly. The war drum and the war horn sounded through the land. And the warriors of my people, ten thousand in number, and I as a young boy amongst them, gathered to face the enemy. For days we fought, but of the Moslem derwishes there were many—more than three times our number.

"They had several big guns that thundered, and most of them had rifles. We killed thousands of them, but at last some of them who were on horseback succeeded in cutting us off from our villages, and then they attacked us from all sides. We lay low in the grass, and only rose from time to time to hurl our spears. The derwishes rained bullets on us, until out of ten thousand who began to fight not more than a thousand were left. Late in the afternoon my father called for a final attack. Here and there a man rose to follow him. We formed a wedge, my father leading, and drove through the enemy, but in the fury of the hand-to-hand fight my father was shot through the head and fell dead.

"We cut ourselves off from our pursuers by killing those who dared to come too far, and escaped into the swamp, and now those devils in human form went to our villages, they took our horses and cattle, they took our mothers, they took our sisters. They took the daughters of the old and the wives of the young, and made slaves of them. They took my mother and my sisters";—and as he said it, tears welled up in the strong man's eyes, for they are a morally clean living people, and the fate of the women

Devils in human form.

and daughters of the tribe had been a cruel one.

"My two young sisters," repeated the chief, "and my dear mother; would they were dead!"

It was trying to see the grief of a strong man, who knew his mother, the honoured one of his father's home, degraded to the level of a beast.

The chief continued.

"The following year after our defeat the Moslems came again, but this time we were carefully prepared for them. We drove a small herd of oxen in front of them to attract their attention. We drove them along a causeway into a swamp, and we lay in ambush. The Derwishes came. They passed us, entered the swamp, when we fell on them, and that day we bathed in blood. We slew them, we routed them, we were like wild beasts, and since then there has never again been a Derwish army in our land. We were free.

"And now you white men have come, and have made peace in the land. You were too strong for the Derwishes, you are too strong for us. You are making roads, you are sending us Moslems to build 'strong houses,' and have Moslems to work the 'speaking wire,' and others to trade with my people. The Moslems build their mosques in my villages, they have become the 'big men' among my people, and soon we shall be their slaves. My young braves have begun to wear Moslem clothes—Moslem fetters. They go with their teachers to the

We shall be their Slaves.

mosque. The Moslems take the young girls of the villages and degrade them."

And for the first time on this journey across the Continent I was definitely asked for religious Christian teachers in the following words:—

"Christian, will you not send us a man to teach us how to worship the great God Who has made you what you are?"

On my return to Khartum I submitted this request to Bishop Gwynne, the Protestant English Bishop of the capital of the Eastern Sudan, but Bishop Gwynne said he had neither men nor means to establish a mission station amongst the Bongo. He expressed his view that the advance of Mohammedanism amongst all these pagan tribes was exceedingly serious, and that something should be done, and done right soon to hinder it. *Bishop Gwynne of Khartum.*

To revert for a moment to the Bongos. When I left their country I was accompanied by some twenty to thirty men of the tribe. The chief came to say good-bye, repeating his previous request for a teacher. Clean limbed, strong and happy fellows these Bongos were. Banter and laughter sounded continually from their ranks. Now they would race each other with their loads on their heads, leaping over the bushes like wild buck, now one of them would perpetrate a specially delightful joke, and the neighbours would sit down by the road, put their loads away, and curl themselves up with laughter. The heaviest loads would go from head to head. All shared each others' burdens, and the "pipe of peace" was common property. When they said goodbye just before we reached Rumbeck, where I changed my carriers, they brought me presents. Three brought their wild cat quivers, three an arrow each, one brought a knife, and another an iron bracelet. They were no beggars, but could afford to give presents. Alas, all European presents had long since been given away by me, and there was nothing left but money. And money seemed to be such a very poor return for the thoughtfulness of my friends. Are not these Bongos to be won for our Christian faith? They are well worth winning, in spite of their reduced numbers.

Well worth Winning.

The greatest Christian missionary pageant the world has ever seen took place recently (June, 1910), in Edinburgh. I had seen the Houses of Parliament in England, the Reichstag in Berlin, the Parliament in Paris, the House of Representatives and the Senate in Washington, but the remarkable World's Foreign Missionary Conference was composed of even more remarkable statesmen than are found in the previously mentioned national assemblies. The assembly was international, composed of the chiefs of missionary enterprise; the heads of the evangelical churches of the world; two Archbishops, sixteen bishops, moderators, conveners, and presidents; leading educationists of the east and the west and the south; professors, lecturers of universities, seminaries, and religious institutions; representatives from Yale and Harvard in the west; and the Minister of Education of Korea from the Far East: from Stellenbosch in South Africa, and the academies of northern Europe. And, lastly, there were administrators there, Government representatives from India and China, from Africa and America, from the Continent and London town.

There were present at that Conference in Edinburgh some of the highest intelligence of the world, the deepest devotion, spiritual dynamite sufficient to meet many of the problems of the world of to-day. It was a most remarkable gathering.

Spiritual Dynamite.

National and race hatred was conspicuous by its absence; multitudes of various denominations representing a host of divergent opinions were welded into harmony.

A long white-bearded high-caste Hindu sat next to an inky-faced negro, and a man in evening dress followed a speaker clothed in the hairy robes of the monks. A pig-tailed Chinese, in flowing silk, rubbed shoulders with a hypermodernised Japanese. But on all faces was the imprint of high mental acumen. Minds there were many, but the souls seemed all centred in One, the Christ, and His glory filled the temple. It was a fore-shadowing of the day that is yet to be when they shall come from the east and from the west, and from the north and from the south, and sit down with the Christ at the last great World's Conference, the preliminary of the federation of the world.

In two words the messages and issues of the Conference might be conveyed. The first word "UNION," the second word "CRISIS." All agreed to differ in minor points, but all were one, without a dissenting voice in the main essentials. And from the Archbishop of Canterbury to the least missionary secretary, the longing, the expectation, the hope and the desire for more perfect inward unity and harmony in co-operation were expressed.

Union Crisis !

But unity was not sought in uniformity of outward dress, of ceremonies or ceremonial, of methods or means; but in the inner working, in cause and effect, all were part of the "ecclesia," of the body of Christ, and necessary.

When on a visit to South Africa some time ago, I had the privilege of speaking to audiences of both Briton and Boer, I found my vocabulary in the Tal language, the language of the peasants of South Africa, somewhat limited, and only consisting of the sentence, "*Kanit verstahn*" (I do not understand.) Before arriving in South Africa it had been impossible for me to understand the political and religious problems of that country, and my only sentence in the language of the people expressed exactly my state of mind. "*Kanit verstahn.*" But to this limited vocabulary I was able to add during the visit another sentence, and on this latter sentence I founded my farewell address in Cape Town. The Moderator of the Dutch Reformed Church, who was in the chair, when asked by me whether

Kanit verstahn.

my pronunciation of the sentence was correct, replied it was quite correct, and when, on further asking whether this sentence would solve the problems and difficulties of South Africa, I was told Yes, this sentence would solve the problems and difficulties of South Africa, and of the world, I made bold to give it to the people, and this was the sentence:

"*Eendragt makt Macht*"—(In union there is strength.) Thank God for a United South Africa of to-day. Thank God for the "Union" manifesto at the World's Missionary Conference.

<small>Eendragt makt Macht.</small>

The second word characterising that Conference is crisis, and there were two crises; one crisis in the East, and the other crisis in the South.

The Eastern crisis, overwhelmingly great, presents the problem, whether the lands of the rising sun, Japan, Korea, China, India, containing more than half the population of the globe, the great heathen masses of the world, like an old giant rising out of the sleep of the ages, who shakes his limbs resulting in national earthquakes, who in wonderment opens his eyes on modern civilisation, and appreciating its value, appropriates it; freeing himself from the restraint of heathen religions that fettered him in his sleep, and with no other restraint, will not constitute the most serious danger that the Christian nations of the world will have to face within the next few years. European civilisation without moral restraint is like a two-edged dagger in the hands of an infant. The problem of the East is

P

serious. Education will not meet it, politics will not meet it, warfare will not meet it, Christ and Christian moral restraint will; Christ, and Christian moral restraint, and nothing else. The "*yellow peril*," the bogey of the German Emperor, is not a bogey but a real thing. The Eastern giant you can hear murmuring to himself in the words of the book, "Ye have taken away the gods which I made, and the priest, and what have I more?"

The yellow Peril.

But yesterday a Chinese staying in the same house with me expressed himself in the following way. "We were quite content with the religions of our country. I have lived in England for sixteen years, and Christianity is a sham." Modern civilisation has taken away the faith in his gods, modern civilisation has defaced for him Christianity at home.

When a few years ago I met the son of a great Indian chief on board an Austrian-Lloyd steamer crossing the Mediterranean, the following conversation ensued:

"You do not look well."

"No, I am dying."

"I am sorry to hear it. What is the matter with you?"

"Tuberculosis. That is all the good that England did to me. I came to study in England. I was a religious man, but religion was taken away from me in England. I was taught to drink. They liked my money, but they did not want to receive me into their homes. You talk about your clean, free women. I have seen no clean women in England. I came as a strong man, and I go away to die."

"What a sordid picture to draw," I can hear from the reader. And yet the incident is perfectly true and a typical incident. We are taking away the gods they have made, and our gifts we bestow upon them are drink, civilisation void of religion, opium, and maxim guns. God have pity on us as a people. The crisis in the East cannot be over-estimated, and the missionaries there have a problem to face that is super-human. **A Sordid Picture.**

So, of course, you may say, is every religious problem, but the Eastern problem is especially so. We are like children attempting to hold down the ocean tide with sand on the seashore. The sand will sink, and the tide will rise, and humanly speaking our labour will be in vain. With men it is impossible, but, of course, there is God. . .

The second crisis, the crisis in the south, constitutes the "*green peril.*" The World's Foreign Missionary Conference placed the position of affairs in Central Africa in their proper relief. The Chairman of Commission I., Dr. Robson, of Edinburgh, when giving the Introductory address on that Commission, stated that the advance of Mohammedanism in Central Africa was so rapid and continuous that unless we were enabled to throw a line of stations right across Central Africa along the border of this Moslem advance, the greater part of Africa would be won for the Mohammedan religion, and that before long. The writer, who was then asked to give an **The Green Peril.**

address on this advance, gave the names of a large number of the unreached pagan tribes along the fore-named border lands, and pointed out that a legion of two hundred spiritual frontiersmen could, humanly speaking, yet stay this advance of the Crescent faith; but that the unreached pagan regions would have to be occupied soon, or we should lose them.

The problem in Africa, unlike the Eastern problem, is a comparatively simple one, and can be met. "The blacker the shame to us if we fail to meet it."

While Americans and our friends on the Continent may assist in shaping the destiny of the tribes in Central Africa, the onus, the burden of responsibility rests upon the British. Shall we call it a burden, or shall we look upon it as a privilege?

An illustration given by a Chinese representative at the World's Missionary Conference sketched an oft-forgotten truth.

The Chinaman's Parable. A little Chinese girl was going along a street with her baby brother on her back. The baby seemed very heavy and the girl very weak. A kind man, coming along the road, and seeing the heavily-weighted child, enquired with solicitude,

"My little one, you must find your burden very heavy?"

The child looked at him, not realising what was meant. The man repeated his question.

"Little one, you must find your burden *very heavy*?"

Still no answer, beyond a further enquiring look.

A third time the interrogation reached the little girl's ear.

" You must find that *burden very heavy?* "

" Burden? Why, he is my brother."

Shall we say because a multitude of heathen tribes are entrusted to us that we get tired of the burden? Nay; rather let us be proud of our trust and shoulder the responsibility gladly.

The spiritual slavery of Mohammedanism is enveloping the tribes in Africa, and war and bloodshed will probably result from it. As I traversed last year the uninhabited wilderness surrounding Sinussi's country, denuded of human life by Moslem slave raids, I could not but wonder what the future may have in store for many of the free clans of Africa.

" Slavery, the earth-born Cyclops, fellest of the giant brood,
  Sons of brutish Force and Darkness, who have drenched the earth with blood,
  Famished in his self-made desert, blinded by our purer day,
  Gropes in yet unblasted regions for his miserable prey;
  Shall we guide his gory fingers where our helpless children play?

" Careless seems the great Avenger: history's pages but record
  One death-grapple in the darkness 'twixt old systems and the Word;
  Truth for ever on the scaffold, Wrong for ever on the throne—
  Yet that scaffold sways the future, and behind the dim unknown
  Standeth God within the shadow, keeping watch above His own."

The end of this Age.

The world's shrinkage, the rate at which history is made to-day, points to the end of this age. It was held by some of the most enthusiastic leaders of modern missionary enterprise, such men as Mr. Hudson Taylor, Dr. Grattan Guinness, and others, that the millennium is near at hand, that the return of the Christ is approaching.

The crisis in the East, the crisis in the South has come. There is no doubt that they will have to be faced, they will have passed within the next ten or twenty years. The Gospel will then, humanly speaking, have been preached amongst all nations as a witness. And then ? . . .

Strategic Points of the Sudan

Sir A. Conan Doyle, in welcoming Booker Washington to London, told of a negro orator, who said that for perfect music on a piano or organ both the black and the white notes would have to be used, and, then, with a burst of enthusiasm, exclaimed, "Yes, and the black notes are on the top." By all means let the best be on the top, but let all co-operate in perfect harmony.

CHAPTER XII

THE Right Hon. Mr. James Bryce, British Ambassador to the United States, gave expression to the following remarkable words at a meeting recently convened by the American Laymen's Missionary Movement in Washington:—

"The moment in which we are now living is a critical moment, or, perhaps, the most critical moment there has been in the history of the non-Christian races. In this time of ours the European races have obtained the control of nearly the whole world, and the influence over even those parts of the world in which they do not exercise political control. Our material civilisation is permeating every part of the world, and telling as it never told before upon every one of the non-Christian races.

"It is transforming the conditions of their lives. They, in their countries, are being exploited as never before, and means of transportation are being introduced as they never were before, which enable foreigners to pass freely among them, and which are completely breaking up and

The Critical Moment.

destroying old organisation and civilisation, such as it was, that existed among them. Under this shock, not only the material conditions of their life, but also their traditions and beliefs, their old customs, and everything that was associated with them, and depended upon their beliefs and customs, are rapidly crumbling away and disappearing.

"What I want to put to you is the supreme importance at this moment of our doing what we can to fill that void which we have made, to give them something to live by instead of that by which they have lived heretofore. Now, when the old things are passing away from them, is the time for us to give them something new and something better by which they may live, through which they may come again into a better progress than they ever could do in their ancient ways. This is the time for us to give them the one supreme gift which the world has ever received, and in which we believe the safety and future hope of the world lie—a knowledge of the life and teaching of our Lord Jesus Christ. This is what we are called upon to give them ."

What the Munchis are in Northern Nigeria, the Musguns are in German Adamawa, the Sara-Kabba in the French Shari Chad Protectorate, and the Nyam-Nyam in the Anglo-Egyptian Sudan; unbroken tribes, clean living, independent masters of the soil. Like our Saxon forefathers, they cannot bear au autocratic rule over them; each family, homestead, or village is practically

STRATEGIC POINTS OF THE SUDAN

independent, and only combines with the next in hunting expeditions or in war-time. When the great battle-drum sounds through the land, the people gather, the elders choose the battle-lord, the dux, the leader, and to him all render implicit obedience.

In physique these four strong tribes are also remarkable. The average height of the men is well over six feet. Most of them will not wear clothes. They call them fetters of slaves. "We do not need to hide uncleanness; we are clean," seems to be their thought.

Four Strategic Points.

These negro nations, children at the present moment, have in them all the essential African attributes and qualities. The Munchis, Musgun, Sara-Kabba, and Nyam-Nyam, therefore, form four strategic points along the advance line of Mohammedanism. There should be no difficulty in winning them for the Christian faith, but only such missionaries should be sent to them as can command their respect physically and ethically. Missionaries to these tribes must be leaders of men, men with a strong will and intellect. Unless such men are sent may none be sent, for weak men who cannot secure the respect of these people will lower the white man's prestige. Manly men and spiritually-muscular missionaries will secure the confidence and the Christianisation of these noblest of the negroes. God grant it may be so.

Let us now consider the aforementioned tribes somewhat more carefully. Not one of them is reached at the present moment by Christian missionaries.

The Munchis. Firstly, we have the Munchis in Northern Nigeria, living on both banks, but mostly on the south side of the Benué, between Lokoja and Ibi. They are estimated at half a million souls. Their largest village on the Benué is Abinshi, and their capital on the Katsena river is Katsena-Alla. The Munchis are agriculturists, but they are also famous hunters. Strong, straight, bold men and women, they live in their clearings in the forest. Certain parts of their land are covered by dense bush, through which narrow zigzag paths have been cut. Moslem traders, who came to Abinshi many years ago, have only been allowed to stay there as long as they remained outside the Munchi village. They are there on sufferance. The Hausa and Fulani are afraid of crocodiles. But as for the Munchis, I have seen them march straight through the Benué in the dry season up to their necks in water, when there were crocodiles all round. They are fearless.

The Niger Company had established trading posts at Abinshi and Katsena-Alla, but the Munchis fell out with the representative of the **Appropriating iron.** Niger Company, and the Niger Company had to withdraw. In the last Munchi rising, the Sudan United Mission happened to have a few hundred sheets of corrugated iron lying on the Abinshi beach. This iron was on its way up to Rock Station. The Munchis were displeased with the agent of the Niger Company, so they burnt down his premises, and as the corrugated iron of the Mission lay close by, they appropriated it and carried it away into the interior to turn it into knives, spear-heads, tomahawks, and swords. Since Northern Nigeria has become a Crown Colony the Government has been compelled to deal with the Munchis. There have been several fights, but nothing very satisfactory has ensued. At the present moment the British Government has a station at Katsena-Alla, but they are there very much as the Niger Company was before them, that is to say, on sufferance.

The second tribe, remarkable on account of its physical, moral, and intellectual qualities, is the Musgun. The Musgun territory is like a wedge driven in between Mohammedan Bornu, Fulani Adamawa, and the slave-raiding Sultanate of Bagirmi. Surrounded by Mohammedans, the Musgun have never been conquered. They are very clever architects, living in remarkable mud buildings, six or seven of which usually form a fort-like compound, the home of the family. Time and time again the Fulanis and Bagirmis have been beaten by the Musguns, who, armed with heavy swords, iron boomerangs, shovel-headed spears, and shields of wicker-work and ox-skin, have not only been able to hold their own, but very often to get the better of the Mohammedan invaders.

Musgun Victors.

The third large tribe of the Sudan is the Sara-Kabba, whose beak-faced women have probably given rise in the Middle Ages to the fables of the dog-headed humans of Central Africa. Lips protruding some six inches amongst the middle-aged women, and the name applied to this people by the Arabs, "Aulad-el-kelb" (children of the dog), are sufficient explanation of the beak-faced people on our maps of the sixteenth century. Were it not for their frightful disfigurement, the young women of the Sara-Kabba might lay claim to physical beauty. They are exceptionally tall. Two of the hunters from that tribe who accompanied me for several days were, if I am not mistaken, six foot six and six foot eight. The Sara-Kabba have a civilisation of their own. Their agricultural implements are different from those of the other tribes of the Sudan. Five hundred years ago they probably owned the whole of the Shari Valley. Then the Bagirmi people came, and later the Fulanis, and lastly, the Arabs and Hausas. The Sara withdrew themselves from the more open country in the north, and from the banks of the Shari, and found refuge in the vast bush and forest region of the Bahr Sara and the Bahr-el-Auk. Many of their towns and villages have never yet been visited by white people, and one can only form a rough estimate of the present size of the tribe, which may be anything between five hundred thousand and a couple of millions; it may be more, or it may be less.

The fourth and last of the great tribes of the Sudan is the Nyam-Nyam. The Nyam-Nyam forms a family of tribes, including a number of little-known clans on the watershed of the Nile and the Congo. The name Nyam-Nyam, produced by the smacking of the lips, was given to the people by the Arabs from the north, and is supposed to denote cannibalism. The natives themselves do not use the word Nyam-Nyam, and those who know it pronounce it Niyamáiyam. The farms of these Nile-Congo watershed tribes are different from those of the former tribes, who lay out large clearings in the bush, on which they plant their millet and their maize. The Nyam-Nyam hoe the ground between the trees, and plant their Kaffir corn in the middle of the forest without attempting to lay out open fields. The Lado Enclave, which has lately been taken back from the Belgian Congo, and added again to the Anglo-Egyptian Sudan, has become the entrance gate to the Nyam-Nyam, opened for the Mohammedan trader, soldier, Government official, and Mualim.

"*Y' Allah! ya ibn el kelb.*" (Go, you son of a dog). There are three things to which the term, "Son of a dog," is applied freely by Arabs, and those three things, are donkeys, slaves, and Christians.

"*Y' Allah! ya ibn el kelb!*"—Whack! and the swinging chastisement fell upon the back of a little heavily-laden donkey. "*Y' Allah! ya ibn el kelb!*" The old white-bearded man, bent by age, drove before him the little beast loaded with all his possessions. The donkey was led by the hand of a small boy clothed only in a narrow strip of loincloth, and behind them followed men, women and children, a motley crowd of some fifty pilgrims, and five other donkeys. A procession in rags and tatters; but a procession solemn and stately. There appeared no laughter and no mirth on anybody's face. There was no song in their mouths, and even the little boys had forgotten how to play. One little fellow whom I employed later to catch butterflies did so in a most serious manner. It looked so unnatural to see a boy of ten years of age with never a smile on his face.

Mecca Pilgrims. The procession we had come upon in the Central African bush was a Mecca pilgrim caravan. Before leaving Fort Archambult two days in advance of us, they had asked permission to accompany us to the Nile Valley, and profit by my protection. These pilgrims seemed desperately poor, and naturally I hesitated to burden my own people with the care of old men, women and children, who might, while traversing the unexplored, be exposed to famine and danger from the natives. I suggested to them that they had better go through the great Moslem States in the Northern Sudan, but there was war up yonder, and the way blocked, and this little beggar caravan was in a pitiful state of destitution. We were travelling at that time through the French Shari Chad Protectorate, having crossed German Adamawa, and these pilgrims came from our own country of Northern Nigeria, and therefore seemed to have a special claim upon us. My own stalwarts, headmen, carriers and boys expressed their wish that we should let the poor people come with us. And with serious misgivings I gave way.

Later, when passing through the uninhabited country between Dar-Kuti and the Bahr-el-Ghazal Province, it seemed that the whole caravan would have died of starvation. Several almost impassable rivers, of which the Kotto was the largest, blocked our way, and it took days to cross them. We were at the end of the rainy season and the grass was very high, so that stalking game was practically impossible. The game would hear the hunter coming while still a long way off, as he broke his way through elephant grass. For over a hundred miles round there was nothing but pathless, foodless bush; the ground was sodden with the rain, the nights were wet and cold. Repeatedly all the fires were extinguished by the drenching rain. One of the old pilgrims died, and we buried him on the bank of a little brook. His only son, a young boy of sixteen, wept over his father's grave. A last farewell look at the little sand mound, and we struggled on again, till at last we reached inhabited regions, the land of food. The first foot spoors of Adam's children were the hieroglyphics of hope to hopeless wanderers in the wilderness.

Pathless, foodless bush.

On the day of our arrival in the first village in the Anglo-Egyptian Sudan a baby boy was born in the caravan, so that the same number of pilgrims arrived in the Nile regions that had left the Shari with me.

I had not seen the pilgrims laugh during the months they had been with me, but when we reached the Nile country, and they came to say farewell, their features were wreathed in smiles, and when I shook hands with them, the faces of the two leaders of the caravan bent down, and their foreheads touched my hand in token of homage. I dislike these manifestations, but they showed gratefulness and affection in these simple children of nature.

From wealth to beggary.
All Mecca pilgrim caravans are not as successful as the one that came with me. Another caravan that had left the Shari Valley six weeks before us, led by the eldest son of the Sultan of Timbuktu, a young man who had made friends with me, was found again by us at Keffi Genji in a pitiable plight. He had lost two-thirds of his people, and a large number of cattle, donkeys, and horses; he had left the Shari a wealthy man; he arrived on the Nile a beggar.

At Fort Archambault, about once a week during the dry season, Mecca caravans appear from the west on their way to their promised land. They number usually from fifty to a hundred and fifty men, women and children, many of them old men that have saved up all their lives that they may go. They start out as caravans, but they come back in units or by twos and threes, lean, shy-eyed undeceived fanatics; the others have gone to their graves. They wait by the side of the way.

"The feet of the pilgrims throng thick on the highway,
  Of mountain and desert and river and plain,
Where heart-weary millions cross country and ocean,
  Benares and Mecca and Heaven to gain."

The good honest men and simple women usually die, and it is only the sly and wiry masters of their fellows that return. The people have a saying that a man who has once been to Mecca is a thief; a man who has returned twice thence is a murderer; but a man who has been three times, watch out for him.

These Mecca pilgrim caravans were up till lately compelled to traverse the Sahara or Northern Moslem States of the Sudan on their way to Arabia. Since the European occupation of the pagan regions, they are enabled now freely to cross the lands of the heathen tribes, and they are availing themselves of this opportunity of travelling by an easier road through a richer country, and at the same time, especially those returning from Mecca, of spreading the religion of the false prophet.

"It cannot be denied," says Captain Cornet, who spent three years in the Lake Chad region, "that in the French possessions in Africa, Mohammedanism advances southwards towards the Gulf of Guinea through the Horse-Shoe bend of the Niger; towards the Congo, through the Shari region, through Bornu and the Sultanate of Dar-Kuti. Nevertheless, there is at present no reason why we should be disturbed by this advance. Fanaticism does not at the present

Elements that may produce trouble.

moment exist in most of these countries. Nevertheless, there are elements that may produce trouble, and in which it is necessary to watch the Marabuts, whose religious influence easily unbalances the minds of the natives.

"The advance of Mohammedanism follows the commercial advance. There is no doubt that it makes use of slavery, but it is the business of our Government to suppress this, and only authorise the exploitation of natural resources."

Bishop Gwynne.

Bishop Gwynne, of Khartum, says Islam is spreading like weeds. In the Western Sudan it spreads in the manner of waves, advancing, returning, but ever progressing; and in the Central Sudan it runs like wildfire; weeds, waves and wildfire.

To the Arab and the Fulah, propagandism is the means to an end; the conversion to Islam and the enrichment of the propagandists should be, of course, synonymous.

Dr. Hugo Zoller.

Dr. Hugo Zöller expresses his views in almost similar terms, though, like others, he admits that, in outward respects, Mohammedanism grafts improvements on the pagan. He says* there is no greater promoter of barbarism in Africa than Islam.

Dr Oscar Lenz.

Dr. Oscar Lenz, on the other hand, states† that Islam is an enemy to all progress, as compared with European standards, and that it exists by reason of its own inertia when left

---

* "Die Deutschen Besitzungen," &c., iii., p. 93.
† "Timbuktu," vol. ii., p. 375.

undisturbed (*wenn er völlig intakt bleibt*). The Koran is the Alpha and Omega of the pious Moslem. The result is, religious intolerance, expressed in the most brutal manner to dependents; and accompanying this fanaticism, an unbridled covetousness, often greater than religious intolerance itself. Moreover, lying to and deception of the "Unfaithful" are, according to Dr. Lenz, the direct legacy of Islam to its adherents. His opinion, in short, appears to be that Islam is the greatest enemy to European culture in Africa.

Recognising the advance of Mohammedanism in Africa as the most serious danger for the future development of that continent, in which is bound up the future faith of the British Colonies of the Anglo-Egyptian Sudan, of Uganda, of British East Africa, of Northern Nigeria and Southern Nigeria, of the Gold Coast, of Sierra Leone, of British Central Africa, of Zululand, of Bechuanaland, of Matabeleland, of the new-formed South African Dominion; territories that are in the aggregate much larger than India, that contain most of the youthful nations of the British Empire, that will in the future be made the supply centres for tropical products: cotton, shea butter, ground nuts, kola nuts, ostrich feathers, ivory, ebony and many valuable woods, as well as the source of unmeasured supplies of minerals, tin, copper, gold, diamonds, &c.,—from the political standpoint these resources need safeguarding, and from the Christian standpoint the indigenous nations owning these supplies must be given the

The need for safeguarding.

fundamental principles on which the British Empire is built, the Bible and the faith in Christ.

It is for us to apply our minds to the organisation of the spiritual affairs of those places and peoples so as to ensure their peaceful and permanent development. It is therefore incumbent upon us to occupy strategic positions in Africa that will allay the advance of Mohammedanism or counteract it. From the military standpoint, if a country is invaded by the enemy there are certain keys to a situation that have to be kept clearly in mind, and that have to be fortified and held. These include the arteries of trade, the centres of population, and certain easily-defended elevated positions on which forts should be constructed. In Africa there are certain natural fortresses that have been a hindrance to Mohammedanism, and will, to a certain extent, be a hindrance in the future. These include Abyssinia, with its population of aboriginal Christians; the inaccessible swamps of the Sudd region; and the impenetrable forests in the north-eastern parts of the French and Belgian Congo country. Between these three, a new fortification has been built in the Christian kingdom of Uganda. We need not be afraid that Mohammedanism will break through such fortifications in its march southward.

In East Africa, where Islam has already secured a preliminary footing, it will probably spread, unless the Massai, the Galla, and the Suahili can be reached by a successful Christian missionary enterprise.

It seems almost too late to expect the conversion of these nations to the Christian religion, as large numbers of them, especially amongst the Suahili and the Gallas, are already Mohammedans. On the slopes of Mount Kenia, in the Rift Valley, and in the direction towards Lake Rudolf, the Kikuyu, the Kavirondo, and others are now being evangelised by missionaries. Whether we shall prevent Mohammedanism from permanently getting a foothold between Lake Victoria, Lake Albert Edward, and Tanganyika, and thus getting into the Congo Valley, is problematic.

For the last fifty years, bands of Moslem slave raiders that have lately changed into Moslem trade caravans, have penetrated by this route into the Lualaba regions, but have not yet permanently affected the tribes there.

The Scottish Mission Schools in Nyassaland will safeguard British Central Africa.

"In the South African Dominions, to which at first, in 1743, by the Dutch East India Company, and later, after the abolition of slavery in 1834, Moslems were brought from India, there are altogether at the present moment some 55,000 Moslems. Of these, 15,000 live in Cape Colony, 20,000 in the Transvaal, and 15,000 in Natal, with a few in the Orange River Colony, and less in Swaziland. These figures were submitted to the Conference of Christian Missions from Moslem Lands held in Cairo, Egypt, in April, 1906. They do not seem quite accurate according to a later statement from South Africa, *Islam at the Cape.*

at least for the Transvaal and Natal, which seem to have each of them not more than 5,000 Moslems. The census of 1904, the last available for Cape Colony, reported 22,623 Mohammedans dwelling in the metropolitan areas; three-fourths of those in the Cape Province lived in the Cape Peninsula. Nineteen out of twenty Moslems in Cape Colony may be found within forty miles of either Port Elizabeth or Cape Town, Johannesburg or Durban.

" The followers of Islam in the Cape Provinces are mostly Malays, two out of every three at least; but the great majority of these Malays are of South African birth. The other third of the Islamites in Cape Colony belong mostly to the mixed or Cape coloured race. There are also nine Hottentots, two Fingals, one Kaffir, one Bechuana, and about fifty Europeans (white). In Cape Town the Mohammedans try to assume towards the Christians an air of superiority, of pity and tolerance.

" But they are on the alert to get all that they can for themselves and their religion, and not neglect opportunities to proselytise. There is a decided increase in the Moslem population, especially in the Cape Districts. From 1891 to 1904, in thirteen years, they added to their number 7,524, that is 50 per cent. But the increase is in favour of the men, their proportion being twelve to one. During the same period the Mohammedans made an advance among the Cape coloured people. In 1891 only 10 per cent. of the Moslems,

STRATEGIC POINTS OF THE SUDAN 233

about 1,500, were of this mixed race; in 1904 one-third, over 33 per cent., and the increase in the thirteen years was thus over 500 per cent. We find this increase especially in the western part of Cape Colony, where there is a strong proselytising tendency. White people there have not always had the right attitude towards the coloured people in the past, and other influences, especially the Ethiopian movement that spread there, remain.

"The mode of the Moslems in increasing their number is rarely that of appealing to reason. Their cause in a Christian land is too weak for that. They have made use of political influence in order to bring Moslem missionaries out to the Cape. They make a practice of taking neglected or abandoned children, and bringing them up in the faith of Islam. Most of these children are of the coloured race, some few are white. **Moslem Methods.**

"There is a movement on foot to establish a college at Claremont which shall become a propagating centre of this faith."

As long as the full tide of Islam from the north does not overflow into South Africa, Moslem propaganda will probably remain limited there. Travelling up the West Coast of Africa from Cape Town we find practically no Moslems in German South-West Africa, practically none in Portuguese West Africa, on the Lower Belgian Congo, on the Lower French Congo, or in the German Kameruns, and we only reach the first **Islam in West Africa.**

outposts again at Lagos. Then we find them on the Gold Coast at Liberia, and Sierra Leone. And in the Senegal they form the bulk of the population.

From all this it appears that from Abyssinia southward East Africa is fairly well guarded. And while Mohammedanism is spreading, and will spread, there appears no likelihood that it will have it all its own way amongst the nations from Uganda to the Cape. In South-West Africa it stands even less chance than in South-East Africa.

But between the Niger territories and the Nile, there is a different story to tell. It is here that the tribes are going. Without a solitary Christian missionary outpost between the Benué region and the Nile, a stretch of 1,500 miles is left unprotected. Our conquest has removed, as already stated, the natural barrier. And the attack is pressed by the most virile branch of the Moslem **Sinussiism.** system, by the modern reform movement of Sinussiism.

What can be done to allay this advance? To begin with, strengthen the present advance posts on the Upper Nile, and in Northern Nigeria. Then send skirmishers ahead, and let certain healthy highlands, inhabited by virile pagans, be occupied. There are three strategic posts. Firstly, the mountain regions south of Lake Chad, from which the low-lying reaches of the Middle Shari might be controlled. This river forms one of the avenues, one of the high roads southward. The second lies on the watershed between the Nile,

STRATEGIC POINTS OF THE SUDAN 235

the Congo, and the Shari system. And the third is in the Southern Hills of Kordofan and Darfur. Access to these three positions is not over difficult.

The first one may be reached by two roads, and it would be well if missions on the Upper Congo, and on the Benué, combined to drive their outposts northwards from the Congo and eastwards from the Benué until they are able to co-operate in the Mountains of Adamawa. The second and third centres must be reached from the Nile, and will probably involve the opening of the last great unexplored waterway in Africa, the Bahr-el-Arab, unexplored by Europeans, but crossed freely by Moslem traders and pilgrims. Both in Northern Nigeria and in the Shari Valley, we have some of the most densely populated districts in Africa. In the Benué, the Shari, with its tributaries the Bahr-Sara and the Bahr-el-Auk, and the Bahr-el-Arab, we have the arteries for present and future commerce of these trade-regions; and in the three strategic points, were they occupied adequately, and fortified, commanding positions that would dominate the centres of population and the high roads of traffic. *[Three strategic points.]*

Here is the plan, workable and effective, if brought into operation. Shall we lose this great objective of the battle-field of modern missions? It involves enterprise worthy of the best. It holds a problem possible of solution. It may be done, it must be done: *[The Plan.]*

" Serrez les rangs. Avant !—Avant ! "*

*The old advance cry of Napoleon Buonaparte for the final attack—" Close the ranks. Forward !—Forward !"

Conclusion:
At Gordon's Statue
The Sphinx

In the purpose of God stands the triumph of Christ;
  The end is assured, for the word hath been spoken;
His promise for yesterday's victory sufficed;
  It holds for to-day, and shall never be broken.
    Forth, then, in faith, be thou faithful to death,
    And expect the fulfilment of all that He saith.
Though against us should rise all the powers of hell,
We hail Thee world's victor, O IMMANUEL!

CHAPTER XIII

WE stood at the foot of Gordon's Statue, Bishop Gwynne, of Khartum, and the writer, behind the Palace Park. The statue's riding-camel's nose high in the air proclaimed indifference to the sweltering heat waves in the silence of the noon-day rest, indifference to the sleepy sons of the Sudan that lay stretched out in the scintillating shadows of the acacia trees. The trappings of the beast were gaudy and gorgeous, setting off the cynical expression of its face.

In the measure in which the animal looked proud and disdainful its rider appeared humble and unassuming, a man with a far-away look.

A man with a far-away look.

It is commonly known in Khartum that the negroes of the poorer classes have begun to look upon the statue of Gordon as semi-divine, for did not Gordon, or, as the natives call him, *Urdun*, die for the people. When these Aulad-el-Abid (children of slaves) have any special petition to bring to the Great Spirit, they go to Gordon's statue, touch their lips with the tips of their fingers, then place their hands on the pedestal of the monument, and believe that the Great Spirit will hear them because of Gordon. A simple rudimentary idea of a mediator.

Waiting for the daybreak.
"Why did they put Gordon at the desert cross-roads, behind the palace instead of in front?" asked the camera-armed tourist of his dragoman (native interpreter).

"White man, they set him looking, not toward the Palace where he lived, nor toward the Nile by which he might have escaped, but toward the Sudan for which he died. He is waiting, sir, for morning to dawn across the Sudan."

He is waiting for the daybreak over the Land of Midnight.

* * * *

For years a feud had been fought between the brave, strong children of the mountains of Central Europe, the liberty-loving sons of snow-clad Switzerland, and the Northern Empire, the Dukes of Austria, a feud so truly depicted in the tales about William Tell. On the one hand, there were the poor, but independent peasants and herdsmen of the hills, and on the other, the steel-clad knights, the gallant, valiant squadrons of the northern plains. Trained in tactics, moulded for the melée, men who had managed the French and mauled the Turks had now turned their faces southward, and had entered the smiling valleys of the wooded uplands of the Alps.

There had been skirmishes before, but now a

steady onward march had begun. What could scythes and short swords accomplish even in the hands of big, powerful men who were only clothed in woollen raiment, against the long joisting lances and iron armour? How can the mountain chamois hurt the hunter? Is there need to tell the story so well known to all, how the field was set, how vainly the Swiss tried to break into the advancing phalanx and failed. What need is there to paint the valiant deed of Arnulf, Arnulf von Winkelried, the Swiss peasant hero, whose sacrifice stands as a lasting monument enshrined in the hearts of a free people.

Arnulf von Winkelried.

"*Was vom Vaterlandsinn der Roemer, von der Spartaner todtverachtenden Mut der Geschichte Griffel berichtet, hier vor Augen, stand es in schoener herrlicher Wahrheit.*"

Swiss would not be serfs. Die they could and die they would, but slaves they never would be. Theirs was the first Republic of modern days, and what the Swiss accomplished in Europe, the Ethiopians, including the Christian Abyssinians and the warlike mountain Pagans, succeeded in doing in Africa. History does not relate the stories of the Arnulfs of Central Africa, but that there have been such there is little doubt. There were those who loved liberty and their homes and people better than life, who gave their lives and gave them gladly. Shall we who, from another continent, as demi-gods have stepped amongst the people of the Sudan, shall we be guilty of indirectly influencing the destiny of free

R

races for evil rather than for good? The pagan clans of Central Africa stand before us as little children.

"Sunt pueri pueri puerilia tractant."

Children they are, and we are their guardians, guardians appointed by God for their good.

*   *   *   *

In the north-east corner of Africa, outside Cairo at the foot of the desert mountains, lies the statue of the riddle-propounding, semi-human, semi-beast-like sphinx, lies there to-day as it lay in the days when Abraham came into Egypt. Half-covered by the drifting sands of the wilderness it lies, its face intently staring eastward.

Waiting for what? Is it waiting for the curse to be removed from the hunted children of Ham, waiting for the sure reward that is yet to come to the descendants and relatives of the cross-bearer of the Christ, waiting for the Lord God of Egypt—Ra—the God of light, the Light of the world?

The riddle-propounding sphinx is in itself a riddle. Bacon regarded this creature as the embodiment of the eternal. Lord Rosebery calls it the most formidable and awesome figure that has ever come from the hand of man.

It is the symbol of Egypt and of Africa, dating from the dawn of time.

CONCLUSION

Thou lookest eastward, for the rising sun—
Half beast, half human; crouching, kneeling low:
With questing eyes that seek the morning glow.
Eternally expectant—Aeons run
Their course and die. Thy task is still begun.
Infinitude thy goal.—By anguished throe
Of endless births the struggling nations grow
From dust to deity, scarce a step is won;
But in thy crouching form and lifted eyes,
Thy brutish body and thy human face,
Turned from the tombs to where the sun must rise,
Is pledged the evolution of the race.
Passion and pain the pathway we have trod,
But from the desert dust we go to God.

L. K.

FINIS

Missionaries in the Sudan

January 1st, 1911

MISSIONARIES IN THE SUDAN.

Missionaries of the Church Missionary Society.

Northern Nigeria.

Alvarez, Mr. Thomas Edgar, M.A., Oxf., to Sierra Leone, 1893; to W. Eq. Africa, 1901; Secretary for Work in Northern Nigeria (St. Peter's, Mowbray, S. Africa).

Upper Niger.

LOKOJA (1865).
    Thomas, Rev. Obadiah, 1896.
    Lacy, Rev. Frederick Hugh, M.A., Camb., 1903. (At Home).

KPATA.
    Williams, Rev. Joshua James, 1896.

BIDA (1900).
    Macintyre, Rev. John Lester, Isl; to W. Eq. Africa, 1896; to Egypt, 1899; to W. Eq. Africa, 1903. (St. Mark's, Sheffield).
    Macintyre, Mrs. J. L., (Mary Jane Greear, to Egypt, 1897; m., 1902). (At Home).

KATSA (1909).
    Ball, Mr. Alfred Ernest, Isl; 1900. (At home).

Hausa States.

ZARIA (1905).

    Miller, Mr. Walter Richard Samuel, M.R.C.S., Eng., L.R.C.P., Lond., 1898.

    Bargery, Rev. George Percy, Isl; 1900. (Exeter G.U. and St. Thomas', Exeter, G.U.). (At home).

    Bargery, Mrs. G. P. (Eliza Minnie Turner, m. 1906). (At home).

KUTA (1906).

    Green, Rev. Leonard Newman, B.A., Cantab. ; 1909.

Bauchi Country.

PANYAM (1907).

    Fox, Rev. George Townshend, M.A., Camb. ; 1907. (Cambridge University Missionary Party).

    Wedgwood, Rev. Charles Henry, B.A., Camb ; 1907. (Cambridge University Missionary Party). (At home).

KABIR (1910).

    Lloyd, Rev. John Whell, B.A., Camb. ; 1906. (Hon. (Cambridge University Missionary Party).

    Fox, Mr. John Crofton, M.R.C.S., Eng. ; L.R.C.P. ; Lond. ; 1909. (Hon.). (Cambridge University Missionary Party).

Northern Sudan.

KHARTUM (1900).

    Work supervised by the Rt. Rev. Llewellyn Henry Gwynne, Bishop of Khartum, who went out as C.M.S. missionary in 1899, and resigned in 1905.

    Bewley, Miss Annie Geraldine, The Olives ; 1903. Girls' School. (Hon.).

OMDURMAN.
> Hall, Mrs. A. C. (Eva Jackson, to Egypt, 1891; m. to the late Dr. Alexander Chorley Hall, 1897), 1891; Girls' School. (Hon.).
>
> Lloyd, Mr. Edmund, B.A., M.B., B.C., Camb.; 1905; ("Living Waters, Miss. Union.")
>
> Jackson, Miss Lilian Verney, 1909.

ATBARA (1908).
> Tristram, Miss Charlotte Jane Josephine, 1908; Girls' School. (Partly Hon.).

Southern Sudan.

MALEK (1906).
> Shaw Rev. Archibald, M.A., Camb.; 1905. (Charles Fox Memorial Fund).
>
> Scamell, Mr. William Hayward, Isl.; 1908. (Archdeaconry of Surrey). (At home).
>
> Lea-Wilson, Rev. C. A., M.A., Camb., 1910.

Missionaries of the Sudan Interior Mission.

PATAGI.

Mr. E. F. Lang	went out in	1894.
Mr. Fred Merryweather	,,	1905.
Mrs. Marion Merryweather (Miss Wutrich).	,,	1905.
Miss S. E. Bender	,,	1909.

WUSHISHI.

Dr. A. P. Stirrett (Field Superintendent).	,,	1902.
Mr. Geo. Sanderson	,,	1908.
Miss M. Witt	,,	1909.

EGBE.
    Mr. Thomas Titcombe   went out in 1908.
    Mr. Rutherford   „ 1909.
KPADA.
    Mr. F. Stanley   „ 1909.
PAIKO.
    Mr. E. F. Rice   „ 1904.
    Mrs. A. Rice   „ 1904.
    Mr. C. E. Dudley   „ 1908.
IKWOI.
    Mr. F. E. Hein   „ 1905.

Missionaries of the Menonite Brethren in Christ.

SHONGA.
    Rev. A. W. Banfield
    Mrs. A. W. Banfield
    Mr. Shirk

JEBBA.
    Two lady missionaries

Missionaries of the Sudan United Mission.

RUMASHA (1908).
    Mr. J. L. Maxwell   first went out 1904.
    Dr. A. G. Alexander, M.R.C.S., L.R.C.P. „ 1908.
    Mrs. Alexander   „ 1909.
    Miss McNaught   „ 1909.
    Mr. G. Dawson   „ 1909.
    Miss G. A. Musgrave   „ 1910.
    Miss C. Haigh   „ 1910.

MISSIONARIES IN THE SUDAN

IBI (1908).

Mr. H. J. Cooper	first went out	1908.
Mr. J. A. Mackinnon	,,	1910.
Mr. D. Forbes	,,	1910.
Mr. W. R. Fleming	,,	1910.

DU (1909).

Rev. E. Evans, B.A.	,,	1908.
Rev. C. Barton, B.A.	,,	1910.

WUKARI (1905).

Rev. C. W. Guinter, B.A.	,,	1906.
Mrs. Guinter	,,	1909.

DONGA (1906).

Rev. C. L. Whitman, B.A.	,,	1910.
Mrs. Whitman	,,	1910.

M'BULA STATION (1909).

Mr. V. H. Hosking	,,	1908.
Mr. J. G. Botha	,,	1908.
Mr. C. F. Zimmerman	,,	1909.

STATIONS TEMPORARILY CLOSED:—

Bukuru	Opened 1907;	closed	1910.	
Langtang	,,	1906	,,	1910.
Dempar	,,	1906	,,	1909.

MISSIONARIES HOME ON FURLOUGH:—

Mr. H. W. Ghey	first went out	1905.
Rev. Paul Barnhardt	,,	1906.
Dr. A. E. Emlyn	,,	1907.
Rev. W. L. Broadbent	,,	1907.

Missionaries of the United Presbyterian Church of America.

KHARTUM. (Opened in 1900).

Rev. J. Kelly Giffen, D.D.	went out in	1900.
Mrs. Grace Giffen	,,	1900.
Rev. George A. Sowash	,,	1903.
Mrs. Katherine Sowash	,,	1903.
Rev. D. S. Oyler	,,	1909.

KHARTUM (NORTH).

Dr. H. T. McLaughlin, M.D.	,,	1900.
Mrs. Lena McLaughlin	,,	1900.
Miss Fanny G. Bradford	,,	1907.
Miss Anna M. Barackman	,,	1909.

DOLEIB HILL.

Dr. Thomas A. Lambie, M.D.	,,	1907.
Mrs. Charlotte Lambie	,,	1909.
Mr. C. B. Cuthrie	,,	1908.
Rev. Elbert McCreery	,,	1906.
Mrs. Hannah McCreery	,,	1906.
Mr. R. W. Tidrick	,,	1906.
Mrs. S. Luella Tidrick	,,	1908.

Bibliography of the Sudan

BIBLIOGRAPHY OF THE SUDAN.

Abudacnus, Josephus.—The true History of the Jocobites of Egypt, Lybia, Nubia, &c., translated by Sir E. Sadler. London, 1892.

Adams, W. H. D. — Egypt, Past and Present and Recent Events in the Soudan. London, 1885.

Adams, W. H. D.—Recent events in the Soudan. London, 1887.

Africa.—Great Explorers of Africa; as told by its Explorers. Two Vols. London, 1894.

Alexander, Lieut. Boyd.—From the Niger to the Nile. Two Vols. London, 1907.

Alford, H. L. S., & Sword, W. D.—The Egyptian Soudan; Its Loss and Recovery. London, 1898.

Alis, Harry. (Hyppolite Percher).—A la conquête du Tchad. Paris, 1891.

Almkvist, H.—Die Bischari-Sprache (Tu-Bedawis) in Nordost Afrika beschreibend und vergleichend, Darge stellt von . . . Upsala, 1881, 1885.

Amelineau, E.—La Géographie de l'Egypte à l'Epoque Copte. Paris, 1893.

Amery, H. F. S.—The Vocabulary of Sudan Arabic, Khartum and Cairo. 1905.

Ampère, J. J. A.—Voyage et Recherches en Egypt et en Nubie. Revue des Deux Mondes. Vols. XV.-XXIII. 1846-8.

Ampère, J. J. A.—Voyage en Egypte et en Nubie. Paris, 1882.

Andre, C.—Forschungsreisen in Arabien und Ost Afrika. Divers Voyages faits par Burton, Speak, Krapf, Rebmann, Eckart, &c. Leipzig, 1861.

Ansorage, W. J.—Under the African Sun. London, 1899.

Archer, T.—The War in Egypt and the Soudan. Four Vols. London, 1885-7.

Archinard, L.—Le Soudan française en 1889-90. Paris, 1891.

Arnaud, Capt.E., et Lieut.M. Cortier.—Mission Arnaud-Cortier. Nos confins Sahariens, étude de géographie militaire. Paris, 1908.

Assenbuch, L. von.—Der Sudanaufstand und die Englische Politik. Unsere Zeit. 1884, hft., 4, 5.

Atteridge, A. H.—Towards Khartoum. The story of the Soudan War of 1896. London, 1897.

Austin, H. H.—Among Swamps and Giants of Equatorial Africa. London, 1902.

Baedeker, K.—Egypt and the Sudan. Handbook for Travellers.

Baikie, W. B.—Narrative of an Exploring Voyage up the River Kwora and Benue in 1854. London, 1856.

Baillaud, E.—Sur les route de Soudan. Toulouse, 1902.

Baker, Sir S. W.—Ismailia ; a Narrative of the Expedition to Central Africa. London, 1874, 1894.

Baker, Sir S. W.—Exploration du Haut Nil. Abrégé par H. Vattemare. Paris, 1880.

Baker, Sir S. W.—L'Afrique Equatoriale. Abrégé par H. Vattermare. Paris, 1880.

Baratieri, O.—Les Anglais au Soudan et la Question d'Abyssinie. Revue des Deux Mondes. Paris, 1899.

Baratti, G.—Travels of G.B. into the Remote Countries of the Abyssinians, or of Ethiopia Interior. London, 1670.

Barges, J. J. P., Abbé.—Le Sahara et le Soudan. Paris, N.D.

Barth, Dr. Henry.—Dr. Balfour Baikie's Thätigkeit am unteren Niger, mit besonderer Berücksichtigung der Flusschwellen dieses Stromes und derjenigen des Tsad-und Nilbeckens. Berlin, N.D.

BIBLIOGRAPHY OF THE SUDAN 257

Barth, Dr. Henry.—Travels and Discoveries in North and Central Africa in the years 1849-55. Five vols. London, 1857.

Barth, Dr. Henry.—Travels and Discoveries in North and Central Africa, including accounts of Tripoli, the Sahara, the remarkable kingdom of Bornu, and the countries around Lake Chad. (Minerva Library). London, 1890.

Barth, Dr. Henry.—Including accounts of Timbuktu, Sokoto, and the basins of the Benué. (Minerva Library), London, 1890.

Bascia, G.—Sette Anni nel Sudan Egiziano. L'Esploratore. 1884.

Bauer, F.—Die Deutsche Niger-Benue-Tsadsee Expedition, 1902-3. Berlin, 1904.

Baumann, O.—Durch Massailand zur Nilquelle, 1891-3. Berlin, 1894.

Baumgarten, J., Ostafrika, der Sudan und das Sudgebiet Land und Leute, &c., Gotha, 1890.

Baylis, F., M.A.—British Nigeria C.M.S. London, 1903.

Beau de Rochas, A.—Oasis et Soudan. Paris, 1888.

Bechet, E.—Cinq ans Séjour au Soudan français. Paris, 1889.

Beke, C. T. —Travels and Researches. London, 1846.

Beke, C. T.—An Inquiry into M. Antoine d'Abbadie's Journey to Kaffa in the years 1843 and 1844 to discover the source of the Nile. London, 1850.

Belzoni, G. B.—Narrative of the Operations and Recent Discoveries in Egypt and Nubia. London, 1820.

Belzoni, C. B.—Voyages en Egypt et en Nubie, &c. Two vols. Paris, 1821.

Belzoni, C. B.—Fruits of the Enterprise exhibited in the Travels of Belzoni in Egypt and Nubia. By Sarah Atkins. London, 1821.

Belzoni, Mrs.—An account of the Women of Egypt, Nubia, &c. Brussels, 1835.

S

Bennett, E. N.—Downfall of the Dervishes. London, 1898.

Berkeley, G. F.—The Campaign of Adowa and the Rise of Menelik. London, 1902.

Bernard, A., and N. Lacroix.—La Pénétration Saharienne (1830-1906). Algiers, 1906.

Besant, A.—The Story of the Soudan. London, 1884.

Bonnetain, Mme. P.—Une Française au Soudan. Paris, 1884.

Bonnetain, P.—Dans la Brousse-Sensations du Soudan. Paris, 1895.

Boteler, T.—Voyage of Discovery to Africa and Arabia. 1821-26. 2 vols. London, 1835.

Bourne, H. R. F.—The Other Side of the Emin Pasha Relief Expedition. London, 1891.

Bowdich, T. E.—Travels in the Interior of Africa. London 1820.

Boyle, St. John.—Travels of an Arab Merchant in the Soudan. Abridged from the French. London, 1845.

Brackenbury, H.—Narrative of the Advance of the River Column of the Nile Expeditionary Force. Edinburgh, 1885.

Brehm, A. E.—Reiseskizzen aus Nord-Ost Afrika—Egypten, Nubien, Sennahr, Roseeres und Cordofahn, 1847-52. Jena, 1855.

Brooks, W. H., and L. N. Nott.—Batu na Abubuan Hausa. With Translation, Vocabulary and Notes. London, 1903.

Brown, A. F.—Report on the Woods and Forests of the Sudan. London, 1902.

Broussais, E.—De Paris au Soudan, Marseille, Alger, Transsaharien. Algiers, 1891.

Brosselard-Faidherbe, Capitaine.—Pénétration au Soudan. Paris, N.D.

Brown. R.—The Story of Africa and its Explorers. Four vols. London, 1883.

BIBLIOGRAPHY OF THE SUDAN 259

Brown, W. G.—Nouveau Voyage dans la Haute et Basse Egypte, la Syrie, le Darfour. Paris, 1800.

Browne, W. G.—Travels in Africa, Egypt, and Syria, 1792-8. London, 1806.

Bruce, J.—An Interesting Narrative of the Travels of J. Bruce into Abyssinia to discover the Source of the Nile. Abridged, with Notes and extracts from the travels of Dr. Shaw, M. Savary, and the Memoirs of Baron de Sott. Boston, 1798,

Bruel, G.—L'Occupation du bassin du Tchad. Moulins, 1902.

Brun-Rollet, N.—Le Nil Blanc et le Soudan. Paris, 1855.

Bryon, Lt. H., and E. B. Macnaghten.—Report on a Recruiting Expedition under Lieut. H. Bryon and E. B. Nacnaghten (1899).

Buchta, R.—Der Sudan unter agyptischer Herrschaft. Leipzig, 1888.

Budge, E. A. W.—On the Orientation of the Pyramids in the Sudan. 1899.

Budge, E. A. W.—Cook's Handbook of Egypt and the Sudan. Second Edition. London, 1906.

Budge, E. A. W.—The Egyptian Sudan. Two Vols. London, 1907.

Burette, H. A.—A Visit to King Theodore. By a Traveller lately returned from Gondar. London, 1868.

Burges, J.—Notice sur le Soudan Français. Paris, 1893.

Burleigh, W. B.—Desert Warfare, being a Chronicle of the Eastern Sudan Campaign. London, 1884.

Burleigh, W. B.—Sirdar and Khalifa. London, 1898.

Burleigh, W. B.—Reconquest of the Soudan. London, 1898.

Burleigh, W. B.—Khartoum Campaign, 1898. London, 1899.

Burney, J.—A Chronological History of North-African Voyages and Discoveries. London, 1819.

Burrow, Capt. G.—The Land of the Pigmies. London, 1898.

Buxton, E. N.—Two African Trips. London, 1902.

Cailiatte, C.—Les Sources du Nil et les dernières explorations dans l'Afrique équotoriale. Paris, N.D.

Cailliaud, F.—Carte detailée du Cours du Nil levée dans l'Expédition de 1819-22. Paris, 1824.

Cailliaud, F.—Voyage à Méroé, &c. Année 1819-22. Paris, 1826.

Cailliaud, F.—Les Abyssiniennes et les Femmes du Soudan Oriental, d'après les relations de Cailliaud, &c. 1876.

Caillié, R.—Travels through Central Africa to Timbuktu, and across the Great Desert to Morocco, in 1824-28. Two vols. London, 1830.

Caillié, R.—Journal d'un Voyage à Timbuctou et à Jenne, dans l'Afrique Central . . . pendant les années 1824-28. Three vols. Paris, 1830.

Caix, De Saint A., Vicomte A. de.—Les intérêts français dans le Soudan Ethiopien. Paris, 1884.

Camperio, Capt. M.—Sette anni nel Sudan Egiziano. (Gessi, R.). Rome, 1891.

Cassati, G.—Ten years in Equatoria. London, 1898.

Chaille-Long, C.—Central Africa ; Naked Truths of Naked People. London, 1876.

Chaille-Long, C.—Niam-Niam à l'Ouest du Nil Blanc. Paris, 1877.

Chatelard, E.—Projet de Colonisation au Soudan. Paris, 1894.

Chavanne, J.—Die Sahara ; oder von Oase zu Oase. Wien, 1879.

Chavanne, J.—Die Mittlere Höhe Afrikas. Wien, 1881.

Chavanne, J.—Afrika im Lichte unserer Tage. Leipzig, 1881.

Chelu, A.—De l'Equateur à la Meditérranée ; Le Nil, le Soudan, l'Egypte. Paris, 1891.

Chesnel, E.—Les Anglais en Egypte ; leurs défaites au Soudan. London, 1887.

Chavalier, A.—Mission Shari-Lac Tchad. 1902-1904. Paris, 1907.

BIBLIOGRAPHY OF THE SUDAN

Chudeau, R.—Missions au Sahara. Two Vols. Paris, 1908-9.

Churchill, W. Spencer.—The River war. Recollections of the Sudan. London, 1902.

Clapperton, H. & D. Denham.—Narrative of Travels and Discoveries in Northern and Central Africa in 1822-24. Boston, 1826. London, 1828.

Clapperton, H.—Journal of a Second Expedition into the Interior of Africa. London, 1829.

Cocheris, J.—Situation Internationale de l'Egypte et du Soudan, juridique et politique. Paris, 1903.

Colborne, Col. Hon. J.—With Hicks Pasha in the Soudan. London, 1884

Collin, V.—La Question du Haut Nile au Point de vue Belge. Bruxelles, 1899.

Colston, Col. R. E.—Reconnaissance from Berenice to Berber. Cairo, 1874.

Colville, Col.—History of the Sudan Campaign, 1884-5. Two vols. War Office, London, 1889.

Colville, Col.—The Land of the Nile Springs. London, 1895.

Combes, E.—Voyage en Egypte, en Nubie, dans le désert de Bayouda des Bischarys. Paris, 1846.

Comyn, D. C. E. ff.—Service and Sport in the Sudan. London, 1910-1911.

Cooper, J.—The Lost Continent. London, 1875.

Cromer, Lord.—Report on Egypt and the Sudan, published annually, containing facts about the Condition, Finance, Administration, &c., of both countries. Published by the British Government in London. Translations in French and Arabic can be obtained in Cairo.

Crowther, Rev. S.—Journal of an Expedition up the Niger and Tshadda Rivers, undertaken by Macgregor Laird, Esq., in connection with the British Government in 1854. London, 1855.

Czerny, F.—Egypt i Mahdi u Sudani. Krakow, 1884.

Dal Verme, P.—I Dervisci nel Sudan Egiziano. Roma, 1894.

Dandola, E. Viaggio in Egitce, nel Sudan, etc. Milano, 1854.

D'Arenberg, Prince P.—Voyage au Soudan Egyptien. Paris, 1904.

D'Avazac-Macaya, M. A. P.—Études de Géographie critique sur une partie de l'Afrique septentrionale. Paris, 1856.

D'Avezac-Macaya, M. A. P.—Esquisse générale de l'Afrique. Paris, 1837, 1844.

Debono, A.—Fragment d'un Voyage au Saubat (Affluent du Nil blanc). Paris, 1861.

Decorse, T. J.—Mission Chari, Lac-Tchad, 1902-1904, Du Congo au Lac Tchad. Paris, 1906.

De Cosson, Major E. A.—The Cradle of the Blue Nile. London. 1877.

De Crozals, J.—Le Commerce du Sal du Sahara au Soudan. Paris, 1896. Les Peulhs, Étude d'Ethnologie Africaine. Paris, 1883.

De Folleville, C.—Célèbres voyageurs des temps modernes. L'Afrique inconnue et les Sources du Nil. Limoges, 1884.

Deherain, H.—Le Soudan Egyptien sous Mehement Ali. Paris, 1898.

Deherain, H.—Études sur l'Afrique-Soudan, Oriental-Ethiopie. Afrique Equatoriale, Afrique du Sud. Paris, 1904.

Delafosse, M.—Essai sur le peuple et la langue Sara (Bassin du Tchad). Paris, 1898.

Delaire.—Les chemins de fer du Soudan à travers le Sahara. Paris, 1877.

De Lanoye, F.—Le Nil, son Bassin et ses Sources. Paris, 1873.

De La Renaudière, F.—Essais sur le progrès de la géographie de l'intérieur de l'Afrique. Paris, 1826.

De Lature, Count E.—Le Désert et la Soudan. Paris, 1853.

De Lature, Count E.—Mémoire sur le Soudan, &c. Paris, 1855.

BIBLIOGRAPHY OF THE SUDAN

Delevoys.—Enseigne de Vaisseau Delevoys. Second de la Mission L'enfant (1903-1904). En Afrique Centrale (Niger-Benoué-Tshad). Paris, 1906.

Denham, D.—Travels and Discoveries in 1822-24, with a short account of Clapperton's and Lander's Second Journey, 1825-1827. London, 1831.

Denon, V.—Travels in Africa. Three vols. London, 1803.

De Rivoyre, L. D.—Aux Pays du Soudan. Paris, 1885.

Descostes, F.—Au Soudan, 1890-91. Paris, 1893.

Desplagnes, Lieut. L.—La Plateau Central Nigerien. Une Mission archéologique, &c., au Soudan français. Paris, 1907.

Dobinson, Archdeacon.—"Niger Letters," 1899. Seeley and Co., London.

Domergue, A.—Senegal et Soudan. Paris, 1895.

Dominik, Hans.—Vom Atlantik zum Tschadsee. Berlin, 1908.

Dubois, F.—Tumbouctou la Mystérieuse. Paris, 1897.

Du Chaillu, P.—Adventures in the Great Forests of Equatorial Africa. London, 1890.

Duchène, M. A.—La France au lac Tschad. 15th April. 1900. (Questions diplomatiques et coloniales). Paris, 1900.

Dunstan, W. R.—Colonial Reports, Nos. 26 and 59. London, 1904 and 1909.

Dupony, E.—Les Chasses du Soudan. Paris, 1894.

Dupuis, C. E.—A Report upon Lake Tsana and the Rivers of the Eastern Soudan. Cairo, 1904.

Duveyrier, H.—Exploration du Sahara. Les Touaregs du Nord. Paris, 1864.

Duveyrier, H.—Liste de Positions Géographique en Afrique, 1884.

Duvivier, Gén.—Abolition de l'Esclavage, Civilisation du Centre de l'Afrique. Paris, 1845.

Dybowski, J.—La Route du Tchad du Loango au Chari. Paris, 1893.

Emin Bey.—Ueber Sudan und Aequatorial provinz im Sommer. Das Ausland, 1882.

Etherington, S.—Egypt, the Soudan and Central Africa. Edinburgh, 1861.

Faidherbe, L. L. C.—Le Soudan Français. Lille, 1881-5.

Feilhauer, G.—Über die Oberflächenformen und die geologischen Verhältnisse des Westsudan vom Atlantischen Ozean bis zum Niger. Inaugural Dissertation. Borna-Leipzig, 1906.

Felkin, R. W., and Wilson, C. T.—Uganda and the Egyptian Soudan.—London, 1882.

Ferryman, Capt. A. F., Mockler.—Up the Niger. Narrative of Major Claude Macdonald's Mission to the Niger and Benué Rivers, West Africa. London, 1892.

Ferryman, Capt. A. F. Mockler.—British West Africa. Its rise and progress. London, 1900.

Ferryman, Lieut.-Col. A. F. Mockler.—British Nigeria. A geographical and historical description of the British possession adjacent to the Niger River, W. Africa. London, 1902.

Flegel, E.—Lose Blätter aus dem Tagebuche meines Haussa-Freundes und Reisegefährten. Hamburg, 1885.

Flegel, E.—Vom Niger-Benué. Briefe aus Afrika. Leipzig, 1890.

Forbes, F. E.—Dahomey and the Dahomans. London, 1851.

Foureau, F.—Au Sahara. Mes deux missions de 1892 et 1893. Paris, 1897.

Foureau, F.—Mission Saharienne Foureau-Lamy. D'Alger au Congo par le Tchad. Paris, 1902. (1904).

Fowler, Sir J.—Report on the Proposed Railway between Wadi Halfa and Shendy; and the Ship Incline at the First Cataract. Cairo, 1873.

Freydenberg, H.—Étude sur le Tchad et le bassin du Chari. Paris, 1908.

Frobenius, H. — Die Erdgebäude im Sudan Sammlung gemeinverständlicher, wissenschaftlicher Vorträge, &c., Neue Folge. Heft 262. 1866.

Frobenius, H.—Die Heiden-Neger des ägyptischen Sudans. Berlin, 1893.

Fuller, F. W.—Egypt and Hinterland to the Re-opening of the Soudan. London, 1903.

Gallieni, J. S.—Voyage au Soudan Français. Paris, 1885.

Garçon, A.—Guerre du Soudan. 1884.

Garstin, Sir Wm.—Report on the Soudan. (Egypt, No. 5). 1899.

Garstin, Sir Wm. — Report as to Irrigation Projects on the Upper Nile. (Egypt, No. 2). 1901.

Gatelet, A. L. C.—Histoire de la Conquête du Soudan. Paris, 1901.

Gentil, E.—La Chute de l'Empire de Rabah. Paris, 1902.

Gessi, F. Pasha.—Setti anni nel Sudan Egiziano. Milano, 1891.

Gessi, F. Pasha.—Seven years in the Soudan. Collected and edited by his son, Felix Gessi. London, 1892.

Gibbons, Major A. St. Hill.—Africa, from South to North. Two vols. London and New York, 1904.

Gibson, A.—Voyages and Travels. (Vol. II.). London, N.D.

Giffen, T. K.—The Egyptian Soudan, 1906. (Contains the history of the American Mission on the Sobat).

Girouard, Sir P. E. C.—Colonial Report, No. 594, Northern Nigeria. London, 1909.

Gladstone, Rt. Hon. W. E.—Egypt and the Soudan. (Speech, Feb. 12, 1884). London, 1884.

Gleichen, Count A. E. W.—Report on Nile and Country between Dongola, Suakin, Kassala, and Omdurman. W.O.I.D. London, 1898.

Gleichen, Capt. Count.—Handbook of the Sudan. Two vols. London, 1898.

Gleichen, Count A. E. W.—The Anglo-Egyptian Sudan. Two vols. London, 1905.

Goetzen, G. A. Von.—Durch Afrika von Ost nach West. Berlin, 1895.

Goldie, Sir G.—Report by Sir George Goldie on the Niger Sudan Campaign (1897) with Miscellaneous Documents, including the Military Report by Major Arnold. London, N.D.

Gordon, C. G.—Text of General Gordon's Proclamation to the Inhabitants of the Sudan, 1884.

Gordon, C. G.—The Soudan, 1882-1897. London, 1897.

Grant, J.—Cassell's History of the War in the Soudan. London, 1885.

Grant, J. A.—A Walk Across Africa, or, Domestic Scenes from my Nile Journal. London, 1864.

Grant, J. A.—Speke's and Grant's Travels in Africa. London, 1864.

Gray, W., and Staff-Surgeon Dochard.—Travels in Western Africa. London, 1825.

Grogan, E. S., and H. Sharp. From the Cape to Cairo. London, 1900.

Guffarel, B.—Le Senegal et le Soudan français. Paris, 1892.

Guillaumet, E.—Le Soudan en 1894. Paris, 1895.

Guillaumet, E.—Tableaux soudanais. Paris, 1899.

Guilleux, C.—Journal de route de la Mission Saharienne. (Mission Foureau-Lamy). Sahara, Soudan, Lac Tchad Belfort, 1904.

Habert, C.—Au Soudan, Excursion dans l'Ouest Africain. Paris, 1894.

Hall, M.—A Woman's Trek from the Cape to Cairo. London, 1907.

Hall, H. R.—Handbook of Egypt and the Sudan. 11th Ed. London, 1907.

Hamilton, J.—Sinai, the Hedjaz, and Soudan, across the Æthiopian Desert from Suakim to Khartum. London, 1857.

Hartert, E.—Ornithologische Ergebnisse einer Reise in den Niger-Benue Gebieten. Naunburg, 1887.

Hassam, V.—Die Wahrheit über Emin Pasha. Berlin, 1893.

Hazeledine, G. D.—The White Man in Nigeria. London, 1904.

Heawood, G. Geography of Africa. London, 1903.

Henning, G.—Samuel Brown der erste deutsche wissenschaftliche Afrika-Reisende. Beitrag zur Erforschungsgeschichte von West Africa.

Hertslet, Sir E.—The Map of Africa by Treaty. New Edition. London, 1910.

Heuglin, T. von.—Reise nach Abessinien, den Gala Ländern, Ost Sudan, und Chartum in den Jahren 1861 und 1862. Jena, 1868.

Hewitt, Captain J. F. N.—European Settlement on the West Coast of Africa. London, 1862.

Hill, G. B.—Col. Gordon in Central Africa, 1874-1879. London, 1897.

Hilmy, Prince I.—Bibliography of Egypt and the Sudan. Two vols. London, 1886.

Hodgson, W. B.—Notes on Northern Africa, the Sahara, and Soudan in Relation to Ethnology. Languages, &c. New York, 1844.

Hourst, Lieut.—French Enterprise in Africa. The Exploration of the Niger. London, 1898.

Hourst, Lt. de Vaisseau.—Sur le Niger et au Pays des Touaregs. Paris, 1898.

Hutchinson, T. J. -Facts of the Niger, Tshadda and Benué Exploration. London, 1855.

Hutchinson, T. J.—Impression of West Africa. London, 1858.

Jaeger, H.—Kamerun und Sudan. Berlin, 1892.

Jaime, Lt. G.—De Koulikoro à Tombouctou à bord du "Mage," 1889-1890. Paris, 1892.

James, F. L.—Wild Tribes of the Soudan. Second edition. London, 1884.

James, F. L.—The Unknown Horn of Africa. Second edition. London, 1888.

Jean, Lieut. C.—Les Touaregs du Sud-Est, l'Air, leur role dans la politique saharienne. Paris, 1909.

Johnson, T. C.—Sport on the Blue Nile. London, 1903.

Johnston, Sir H.—The Nile Quest. Record of Exploration of the Nile and its basin. London, 1896.

Johnston, H. H.—A Journey up the Cross River. Proceeding of the E.G.S. London, 1888.

Jomard, M.—Notice Historique sur la Vie et les Voyages de Réné Caillié. Paris, 1839.

Jouveaux, E.—Deux ans dans l'Afrique orientale. Tours, 1871.

Julien, Capt.—Le Dar Ouadai (Renseign. Colon. Comitée de l'Afr. Français, 1904. Four arts.).

Junker, Dr. W.—Travels in Africa during the years 1875-1886. Translated from German by A. H. Keane. Three vols. London, 1890-2.

Kingsley, M. H.—Travels in West Africa. London, 1897.

Kingston, W. H. G.—Adventures in Africa by an African Trader. London, 1883.

Kingston, W. H. G.—Great African Travellers. London, 1885.

Kingston, W. H. G.—Travels of Mungo Park, Denham and Clapperton. London, 1886.

Klobb, Lieut.-Col.—Dernier Carnet de Route au Soudan Français. Paris, 1905.

Knight, E. F.—Letters from the Sudan. By the Special Correspondent of the *Times* (E. F. Knight). Reprinted from the *Times* of April to October, 1896. London, 1897.

Kohn-Abrest, G.—L'Expédition anglaise et le Soulèvement du Soudan. La Tripolitaine, 1884.

Kumm, H. K. W.—Tribes of the Nile Valley. Osterode, 1902.

Kumm, H. K. W.—Versuch einer wissenschaftlichen Darstellung der wirtschafts-geographischen Verhältnisse Nubiens von Assuan bis Dongola. Gotha, 1903.

Kumm, H. K. W.—The Sudan : a short Compendium of Facts and Figures about the Land of Darkness. London, 1907.

Kumm, H. K. W.—From Hausaland to Egypt through the Sudan. London, 1910.

Lagrillière, B. E.—Chambres de Commerce : Mission au Sénégal et au Soudan. Paris, 1898.

Laing, Major G. A.—Travels in the Timannee, Kooranko and Soolima Countries in Western Africa. 1825.

Lamb.—Trade of Suakin (Foreign Office Reports).

Lander, R.—Records of Captain Clapperton's last Expedition to Africa, with the subsequent adventures of the Author. Two vols. 1830.

Landor, A. H. S.—Across Widest Africa. Two vols. 1907.

Landor, R. & J.—A Voyage down the Dark River. London, 1832.

Lecerf, P. E.—Lettres du Soudan. Paris, 1895.

Leeder, S. H.—The Desert Gateway. London, 1910.

Le Jean, G.—Les Deux Nils. Paris, 1866.

Lenfant, Commandant.—La grande route du Tchad. Préface par M. Le Myre de Vilers. Introduction de Maurice Albert. Paris, 1905.

Lenfant, Commandant.—La Découverte des sources du Centre Africain. (Mission for Exploration of S. Shari Basin). Paris, 1909.

Lenz, Dr. O.- Skizzen aus Westafrika. Berlin, 1878.

Lenz, Dr. O.—Timbuktu. Reise durch Marokko, die Sahara und den Sudan. 1879-1880. Two Vols. Leipzig, 1884.

Lenz, Dr. O.—Timbouctou. Voyage au Maroc et au Sudan. Paris, 1886.

Leo Africanus, J.—Déscription de l'Afrique. Two vols. Antwerp.

Leo Africanus, J.—Geographical Historie of Africa; before which, out of the best Ancient and Modern Writers, is prefixed a generale description of Africa, and also a particular treatise of all the Main Lands and Isles undescribed by John Leo Africanus. Translated and collected by John Pory. 1600.

Leo Africanus, J. — Pertinente Beschryvinge von Africa, Rotterdam. 1565.

Leo, Africain.—De l'Afrique, contenant le Déscription de ce Pays. Traduction de Jean Temporal. Four vols. Paris, 1830.

Leon, Jean.—Déscription de l'Afrique. Two vols. Lyons, 1556.

Leroy-Beaulieu, P. P.—Le Sahara, le Soudan, et les Chemins-de-fer transahariens. Paris, 1904.

Le Vaillant, F.—Voyage et Second Voyage dans l'intérieur de l'Afrique. 1780-85. Paris, 1780-96.

Leyden, J.—A Historical and Philosophical Sketch of the Discoveries and Settlements of Europeans in Northern and Western Africa. 1799.

Leyden, J.—Historical Account of Discoveries and Travels in Africa. Two vols. Edinburgh, 1817.

Leyden, J.—Histoire Complète des voyages et découvertes en Afrique. Four vols. Paris, 1821.

Light, H.—Travels in Nubia. London, 1818.

Lloyd, A. B.—Uganda to Khartoum. London, 1906.

Lugard, Sir F.—Colonial Reports—
No. 346, Northern Nigeria, 1902.
„ 377 „ „ 1903.
„ 409 „ „ 1903.
„ 437 „ „ 1904.
„ 476 „ „ 1905.
„ 516 „ „ 1907.

Lugard, Lady.—A Tropical Dependency. London, 1905.

Lyon, Capt. G. F. R. N.—A Narrative of Travels in Northern Africa in the years 1818-1820. Geographical Notices of the Soudan, &c. London, 1821.

Macdonald, A.—Too Late for Gordon and Khartoum. London, 1887.

Macdonald, A.—Why Gordon perished, or the causes which led to the Soudan disasters. London, 1896.

Maclaird and Oldfield.—Narratives of an Expedition into the Interior of Africa, 1832-34. London, 1837.

Macmaster, M.—The Egyptian Soudan. London, 1885.

Macmichael, H. A.—Notes on the History of Kordofan before the Egyptian Conquest, 1907. (Extracted from an official report.)

Mage, A. E., and Quintin.—Voyage dans le Soudan occidental. Paris, 1868.

Magyar, L.—Voyages dans l'Afrique du Sud, 1849-57. Paris, 1859.

Maistre, C.—La région du Bahr-Sara. Montpellier, 1902.

Maistre, C.—A Travers l'Afrique Centrale du Congo au Niger. 1892-1893. Paris, 1905.

Mardon, H. W.—A Geography of Egypt and the Anglo-Egyptian Sudan. London, N.D.

Mariette Bey, A.—Déscription des feuilles executées en Egypte, en Nubie, et au Soudan, 1850-54. Paris, 1863-67.

Marno, E.—Reisen im Gebiete des blauen und weissen Nil, im ägyptischen Sudan und den angrenzenden Negerländers in den Jahren, 1869 bis 1873. Wien, 1874.

Marno, E.—Reise in der ägyptischen Aequatorial-Provinz und in Kordofan in den Jahren, 1874-76. Wien, 1879,

Marquardsen, Lt. H.—Die Geographische Erforschung des Tshadsee gebietes bis zu 1905. (Mitt. Deuts. Schutzgebieten, 1905, p.p. 318-347).

Marquardsen.—Oberflächengestalung und Hydrographie des Sahara-Sudanischen abflusslosen Gebietes. Jnaug, Diss., Göttingen, 1909.

Martin, A. G. P.—A la frontière du Maroc. Les Oasis Sahariennes. (Gourara-Touat-Tidikelt). Tome I. Algiers, 1908.

Matthews, G. R.—Colonial Reports No. 633, Northern Nigeria. London, 1910.

Melly, Andre D.—Letters d'Egypte et de Nubie. Sept. 1850, à Janvier, 1851. Privately printed. London, 1852.

Melly, G.—Khartoum and the Blue and White Nile. Two vols. London, 1851.

Mercier, E.—La France dans le Sahara et Soudan. Three tom. Paris, 1888.

Mitterutzner, J. C.—Die Dinka Sprache in Central Afrika. Brixen, 1866.

Monteil, C.—Soudan Français. Lille, 1903.

Monteil, Lieut.-Col. P. L.—De Saint-Louis à Tripoli par le Lac Tchad. Voyage au travers du Soudan et du Sahara accompli pendant les années 1890-92. Paris 1894.

Moore, F.—Travels in the Inland Parts of Africa. London, 1738.

Morel, E. D.—Affairs of West Africa (William Heinemann). London, 1902.

Morgen, C.—Durch Kamerun von Süd nach Nord. Leipzig, 1893.

Mosely, L. H.—Regions of the Benué (the Geographica Journal). Vol. xiv. No. 6. London, 1899.

Mouriez, P.—Histoire de Méhémet Ali (notes sur les mines d'or du Soudan et sur le voyage que fit Méhémet Ali, &c.). Paris, 1857.

Muhammed, Ibn Omar El-Tounsy. Voyage au Darfour. Traduit de l'Arabe par Perron. Préface par. M. Jomard. Paris, 1850.

Muhammed, Ibn Omar El-Tounsy. Voyage au Ouaday. Paris, 1854.

Muriel, E. C.—Report on the Forests of the Soudan. Cairo, 1901.

Murray, H.—Historical Accounts of Discoveries and Travels in Africa, &c. Edinburgh, 1820.

Myers, A. B. R.—Life with the Hamram Arabs, Sporting tour in the Soudan. London, 1876.

Nachtigal, Dr. G.—Sahara und Sudan. Three vols. Berlin, 1879-89.

Nachtigal, Dr. G.—Trauerfeier für Gustav Nachtigal, 17 Mai, 1885. Berlin, 1885.

Neufeld, C.—A Prisoner of the Khalifa. London, 1899.

Nigeria.—Northern Nigeria. Correspondence relating to Kano. London, 1903.

Nigeria, Northern. — Correspondence relating to Sokoto, Hadeija, and the Munshi country. London, 1907.

Norden, F. L.—Travels in Egypt and in Nubia. Two vols. London, 1757

Norden, F. L.—The Antiquities, Natural History, &c., of Egypt, Nubia, and Thebes, from drawings taken on the spot. London, 1792.

Norden, F. L. — New Voyages and Travels. Vol. II. London, 1819.

Oberländer, R.—West Afrika vom Sengal bis Benguela. Leipzig.
Olivier, A., Viscount de Sanderval.—Soudan français. Paris, 1893.
Oppenheim, Dr. M.—Rabeh und das Tschadseegebiet. Berlin, 1902.
Oudney, Dr.—An Outline of the Discoveries in Central Africa made by Dr. Oudney, Major Denham, and Lieut. Clapperton. London, 1825.

Page, J.—Samuel Crowther. London, 1888.
Palat, B. C.—Campagne des Anglais au Soudan. Paris, 1884-5.
Pallme, J.—Travels in Kordofan. Translated from the German. London, 1844.
Park, M.—Travels in the Interior Districts of Africa, performed under the Direction and Patronage of the African Association in the years 1795-1796, and 1797, with an Appendix, containing Geographical Illustrations of Africa, by Major Rennell. Fourth Edition. 1800.
Park, M.—The Journal of a Mission to the Interior of Africa in the year 1805, together with other Documents, Official and Private, relating to the same Mission, to which is prefixed an Account of the Life of Mr. Park. London, 1815.
Park, M.—Travels in Africa. London, 1816.
Park, F. H.—My experiences in Equatorial Africa as Medical Officer of the Emin Pasha Relief Expedition. London, 1898.
Parry, Major E.—Suakin, 1885. London, 1886.
Passarge, S.—Central Sudan. Berlin, 1895.
Passarge, S.—Adamawa; Bericht über die Expedition des Deutschen Kamerun-Komitees in den Jahren 1893-4. Berlin, 1895.

Paulhiac, Lieut. H.—Promenades Lointaines. Sahara, Niger, Tombouctou, Touarek. Preface par Hugues le Roux. Paris, N.D.

Pavel, O.—Meine Expedition zum Tschadsee. Berlin, Deutsches Kolonialblatt, 15th November, 1902, p. 543, 546.

Peel, Hon. S.—The Binding of the Nile and the New Sudan. London, 1904.

Penazzi, L.—Sudan e Abissinia. Bologna, 1885.

Pensa, H.—L'Egypte et le Soudan Egyptien. Paris, 1895.

Peroz, Commandant.—Au Niger. Récits de Campagnes, 1891-2. Paris, 1894.

Perrot, J. F. A.—Essai sur les Momies. Historie Sacrée de l'Egypte et de la Nubie. Nimes, 1844.

Petherick, J.—Egypt, the Soudan and Central Africa. London, 1861.

Pethrick, J.—Travels in Central Africa. Two vols. London, 1869.

Pierre, C. T., and Monteil, C.—L'Esclavage au Soudan. Paris, 1905.

Pimblett, W. M.—Story of the Soudan War. London, 1885.

Pinkerton, J.—Voyages and Travels. Seventeen vols. London, 1808-14.

Please, A. E.—Travel and Sport in Africa. Three vols. London, 1902.

Pommerol, J.—Among the Women of the Sahara. Translated from the French by Arther Bell. London, 1903.

Power, F.—Letters from Khartoum during the Siege. London, 1885.

Prax.—Instruction pour le voyage de M. Prax dans le Soudan Septentrionale. Paris, 1847.

Prins, P.—Vers le Tchad. Une année de residence auprès de Mohamed Abd-er-Rhaman Gaourang Sultan de Bagirmi, Avril, 1898; Mai, 1899. (La Géographie bulletin de la Société de Géographie). Paris, 1900.

Prout, Major H. G.—General Report on the Province of Kordofan. Cairo, 1877.

Purdy, Col. E. S.—Psychometrical Observations taken at Fasher, Darfour, &c. Cairo, 1877.

Reed, J. H.—Fashoda and the Bahr-el-Ghazal. Manchester, 1899.

Repoux, Capt.—Le Ouadai. (Bul. Soc. Commerc. Bordeaux, 1909, pp. 8-15, 23-32).

Reulle, M.—Au Sudan, 1893-94. Reims, 1896.

Richardson, J.—Tour of Nine Months through the Heart of the Great Desert of the Sahara. M.S., Folio, pp. 30 and Second Notice, N.D.

Richardson, J.—Mons. Caillié's Account of Timbuctoo, compared with the Information procured by Mr. J. Richardson during his late Tour through the Great Desert. M.S. Folio. 1847.

Richardson, J.—Travels in the Great Desert of Sahara. Two vols. 1848.

Richardson, J.—Narrative of a Mission to Central Africa in 1850-51. Two vols. 1853.

Rifaud, J. J. — Voyage en Egypte, en Nubie et lieux circonvoisins depuis 1805 jusqu'a 1827. Paris, 1829.

Robinson, C. H.—Hausaland; or, Fifteen Hundred Miles through the Central Soudan. London, 1896.

Robinson, C. H.—Nigeria, our latest Protectorate. London, 1900.

Rohlfs, Dr. G.—Quer durch Afrika. Leipzig, 1854-75.

Romagny, C. M.—Campagnes d'un siècle. Tunis, Soudan, &c. Paris, 1900.

Rosellini, I.—Monumenti dell' Egitto et Nubia. Three vols. Pisa, 1834.

Rosignoli, P.—I miei dodici-anni di prigionia in mezzo dei dervisci del Sudan. Mondovi, 1898.

Rossi, E.—La Nubia e il Sudan. Constantinople, 1858.
Rouget, F.—L'Expansion Coloniale au Congo française. Paris, 1906.
Rowley, H.—Africa Unveiled. London, 1876.
Rowley, H.—Twenty years in Central Africa. London, 1882.
Rueppell, Dr. E.—Zoologischer Atlas zu Reisen im nördlischen Afrika. Frankfurt, 1826.
Rueppell, Dr. E.—Reisen in Nubien, Kordofan un dem petraeschen Arabien. Frankfurt am Main, 1829.
Russel, H.—The Ruin of the Soudan ; cause, effect and remedy. London, 1892.
Ruxton, Capt. F. H.—The Geographical Journal. Vol. XXI. No. 1. London, 1903.

Sabatier, C.—Touat, Sahara, et Soudan. Paris, 1891.
Sanderval, O.—Soudan-Français. Paris, 1893.
Santalena, A,—L'Insurrezione du Sudan. Treviso, 1881-1885.
Sarrazin, H.—Races humaines du Sudan Français. Chambery, 1901.
Sartorius, Mrs. E.—Three Months in the Soudan. London, 1885.
Schauenberg, Dr. E.—Reisen in Central Afrika. Lander, Clapperton, und Mungo Park. 1859.
Schefer, C. H. A., and Cordier.—Recueil de Voyages, &c., Relation de l'Ambassade de D. Trevisan auprès du Sudan à Egypt, 1512. Publié et annoté par C. Schefer. Recueil de Voyages, 1884 ; No. 5, Paris.
Schirmer, H. —Le Dernier rapport d'un Européen sur Ghât et les Touaregs de l'Air. (Journal de Voyage d'Erwin de Bary, 1876-77). Paris, 1898.
Schirmer, H.—Le Sahara. Paris, 1893.
Schoenfeld, E. D.—Erythräa und der ägyptische Sudan. Berlin, 1904.

Schucair, Naum Bey, B. A.—The History of the Geography of the Sudan. Three vols. Cairo, 1903. (In Arabic.)

Schultze, D. A.—Das Sultanat Bornu mit besonderer Berücksichtigung von Deutsch-Bornu. Essen, 1910.

Schweinfurth, G.—Im Herzen von Afrika. Reisen und Entdeckungen im Centralen Aequatorial Afrika, 1868-71, 2. Leipzig, 1874.

Schweinfurth, G. — In the Heart of Africa. Two vols. London, Third edition, 1878.

Schweitzer, C., Schnitzer, E. (Emin Pasha). Berlin, 1898.

Scott-Elliott, G. F.—A Naturalist in Mid-Africa. London, 1896.

Sipp, C.—Central Soudan. Meissen, 1888.

Slatin, Rudolf C.—Fire and Sword in the Soudan. Translated by Major J. R. Wingate. London, 1896.

Slatin, Pasha, Sir R. C.—Feuer und Schwert im Sudan, 1879-95. Leipzig, 1896.

Smith, A. D.—Through Unknown African Countries. London, 1897.

Smith F. H.—Pacification of the Sudan, &c. London, 1887.

Sommerville, M.—Sands of Sahara. Philadelphia, 1901.

Southworth, A. S.—Four Thousand Miles of African Travel. New York and London, 1875.

Speedy, Mrs. C. M.—My Wanderings in the Soudan. Two vols. London, 1884.

Stanford, E.—Compendium of Geography and Travel in Africa. Two vols. By A. H. Keane. London, 1907.

Stanley, Sir H. M.—Through the Dark Continent. London, 1878.

Stanley, Sir H. M.—In Darkest Africa. London, 1890.

Stanley, Sir H. M.—Im Dunkelsten Africa. Two Bds. Leipzig, 1890.

Steevens, G. W.—With Kitchener to Khartum. Second Edition. London, 1898.

BIBLIOGRAPHY OF THE SUDAN

Stephens, J. P.—Notes of Travel in Egypt and Nubia. London, 1876.

Stewart, Col.—Report on the Sudan. Egypt, 1883. No. 11, 1883.

Stuhlmann, Dr. F.—Mit Emin Pasha ins Herz von Afrika. Berlin, 1894.

Sudan, Egyptian.—The Sudan Almanac, Cairo. (Published yearly).

Sudan, Egyptian.—Report on the Egyptian Province of the Soudan. London, 1883.

Sudan, Egyptian.—The True Prophet in the Soudan. London 1885.

Sudan, Egypt, No. 2 (1898).—Correspondence with the French Government respecting the Valley of the Upper Nile. London, 1898.

Sudan, Egypt.—"Sudan Gazette." Published monthly, by authority of the Sudan Government. Cairo. First issue, March 7th, 1899.

Sudan, Egypt.—Sudan Campaign, by "An Officer." London, 1899.

Sudan, Egypt.—Address and Corrigenda for 1902-3, to the Notes for Travellers and Sportsmen in the Sudan.

Sudan, Egypt.—Guide to Egypt and the Sudan. Fifth Edition. London, 1908.

Sudan, French.—Deux Campagnes au Soudan Français, 1886-8. Paris, 1891.

Sudan, French.—Exposition Universelle de 1900. Les Colonies Françaises. Senegal-Soudan. Agriculture, Industrie, &c. Paris, 1900.

Sudan War.—Lives and Adventures of Heroes of the Soudan War. London, 1887.

Sykey, Captain C. A.—Service and Sport on the Tropical Nile. London, 1903.

Tabarie, M.—C. G. Gordon, le défenseur de Khartoum. Paris, 1886.

Tangye, H. L.—In the Torrid Sudan. London, 1910.

Taylor, B.—Life and Landscape from Egypt to the Negro Kingdoms of the White Nile. London, 1854.

Taylor, B.—Eine Reise nach Central Afrika. Leipzig, 1855.

Tellier, K. H.—Etude Soudanaise. Paris, 1902.

Terrier, A.—La Réorganisation du Congo et du Chari. Bulletin du Comité de l'Afrique française. Paris, Août, 1902.

Terrier, A.—Le Massacre de la Mission Bretonnet (Comité de l'Afrique française), p. 362-368, 9 année, No. 11. Paris, 1899.

Thomson, J.—To the Central African Lakes and Back, 1878-80. London, 1881.

Traill, H. W.—From Cairo to the Sudan Frontier. London, 1896.

Traill, H. D.—England, Egypt and the Sudan. London, 1900.

Tremaux, P.—Rapport sur le Voyage au Soudan Oriental. Paris, 1853.

Tremaux, P.—Voyage en Ethiopie, au Sudan Oriental, et dans la Nigritie. Paris, 1862.

Tremearne, Capt. A. J. N.—Niger and the West Sudan. London, 1910.

Trotter, Col. J. K.—The Niger Source. London, 1897.

Ule, Otto.—Sahara und Sudan. Halle, 1861.

Vancelle, L.—Chronologie des Monuments Antiques de la Nubie, &c. Paris, 1829.

Vandeleur, G.—Campaigning on the Upper Nile and the Niger. London, 1898.

Verner, Capt. W.—Sketches in the Soudan. London, 1886.

Vierkandt, Dr. A.—Die Volksdichte im Westlichen Central Africa. Leipzig, 1895.
Vigne, Dr. P.—Terre de Mort Soudan. Paris, 1892.
Vischer, H.—Across the Sahara from Tripoli to Bornu. London, 1910.
Vivarez, M.—Le Soudan Algérien. Paris, 1890.
Vossion, L.—Khartoum et le Soudan d'Egypt. Paris, 1890.
Vossion, L.--Les Provinces Egyptiennes du Soudan et de l'Equateur. Paris, 1892.
Vugliano, C.—Gli ultimi avvenimenti de Sudan Frosinone. 1891.
Vuillot, P.—L'Exploration du Sahara Etude historique et géographique. Préface du Colonel Prince de Polignac. Paris, 1895.

Walkenaer, Baron, C. A.—Récherches Géographiques sur l'Intérieur de l'Afrique Septentrionale. Paris, 1821.
Walkenaer, Baron, C. A.—Collection de relations de voyages par mer et par terre en differentes parties de l'Afrique, depuis 1400 jusqu'à nos jours. Twenty-one vols. Paris, 1826-31.
Wallace, W.—Colonial Report, No. 551, Northern Nigeria. London, 1907.
Ward, J.—Our Sudan, its Pyramids and Progress. London, 1905.
War Office.—Report on the Egyptian Provinces of the Soudan, Red Sea, and Equator. London, 1884.
Watkins, C. S.—With Kitchener's Army; a Chaplain's Experiences with the Nile Expedition. London, 1899.
Watson, Col. Sir C. M.—Comparative vocabularies of the languages spoken at Suakin. London, 1868.
Watson and Chippendall.—Survey of the White Nile. Cairo, 1874.
Werne, F.—Die Völker des Ost Sudan. (N. P. and N. D.).

Werne, F.—Expedition to discover the Sources of the White Nile, 1840-41. Two vols. London, 1849.

Werne, F.—Feldzug von Sennaar nach Taka, Basa, und Beni Amer, &c. Stuttgart, 1851. Also translated into English by J. B. Johnston. London, 1852.

West Africa.—Treaty Series. No. 17, 1906. London, 1906.

Williams, Dr. J.—Life in the Soudan in 1881-82. London, 1884.

Wilson, C. T., and Felkin, R. W.—Uganda and the Egyptian Sudan. London, 1882.

Wilson, Sir C. W.—From Korti to Khartoum. London, 1886.

Wingate, Sir F. R.—Mahdism and the Egyptian Sudan. London, 1891.

Wingate, Sir F. R., and Father Ohrwaldler.—Ten Years' Captivity in the Mahdi's Camp, 1882-92. London, 1892.

Witherby, H. F.—Bird Hunting on the White Nile. A Naturalist's Experiences in the Sudan. London, 1902.

Wolff, H., and Blacker, A.—Sahara et Soudan. Les Régiments de Dromadaires. Paris, 1884.

Wright, H. C. S.—Soudan, 1896. London, 1897.

Wylde, A. B.—1883 to 1887 in the Sudan. Two Vols. London, 1888.

Wyndham-Guin, W. T.—The Soudan, its History, Geography, and Characteristics. A lecture. London, 1884.

Zintgraff, Dr. E.—Nord-Kamerun, Schilderung der im Auftrage des Auswärtigen-Amtes zur Erschliessung des nördlichen Hinterlandes von Kamerun während der Jahre 1886-1892, unternommenen Reisen. Berlin, 1895.

Index

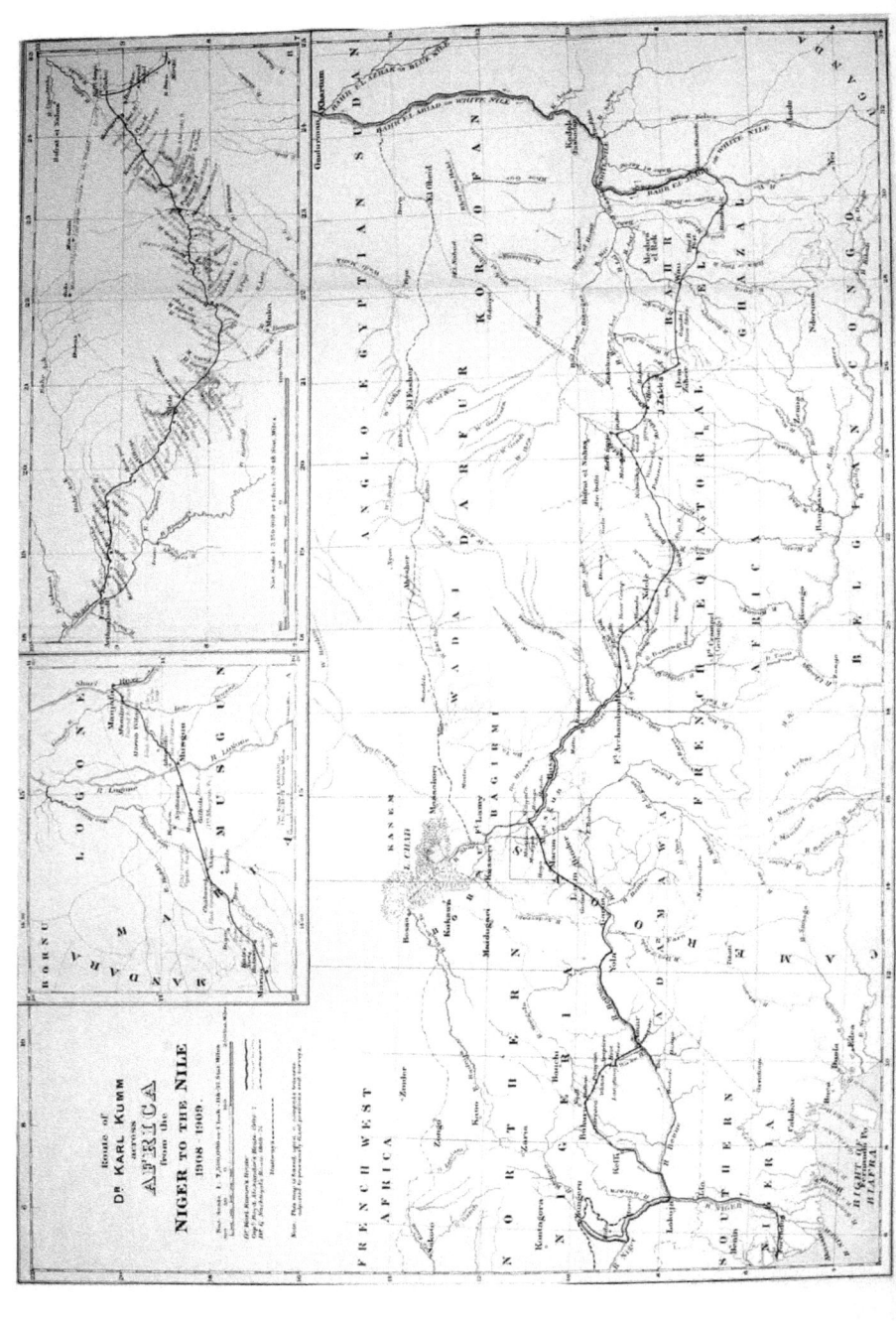

INDEX

	PAGE
ABDUL-HAMID	127
Abd-ul-'Kader	120
Abdulla	117
Abinshi	220
Abu-Bekar	124
Abyssinia	97, 115, 118, 165, 186, 230, 234
Adal	119
Adamawa	29, 35, 36, 83, 99, 100, 102, 121, 132, 221, 235
Africanus, Leo	192
Ahriman	135
Ain-Galakka	131
Air	131
Akba	117
Albert Edward Lake	231
Albert Lake	183
Alexander, Boyd	84
Alexander, Dr. G.	43
Alexandria	116, 160, 161, 186
Algiers	22, 115, 130, 131, 187
American Missionaries	44, 75, 186, 187
Amon	166, 167
Amru	116
Anglo-Saxon	8, 10, 11, 12, 135
Ankwes	48
Antelope	64, 77, 93, 96, 98, 183
Arnot	192
Apostelstrasse	186
Ashantees	147
Assiut	186
Assuan	186

	PAGE
Atbara	166
Atlantic Mt.	140
Audu-Gajere (David)	171, 172, 173, 174, 175
Augustine	10
Axum	166
BA	94, 96
Bacon	242
Baganda	7, 10
Bagirmi	38, 116
Bahr-el-Arab	235
Bahr-el-Auk	222, 235
Bahr-el-Gasahl (ghazal)	38, 201, 225
Bahr-Sara	222, 235
Bamum	98
Banfield	168
Bantu	12, 139, 142
Banza-Manteke	181, 182, 188, 194
Barejuko	40, 41
Barnhardt	154
Baro	39, 43
Baro Kano	39
Barotsi	7, 181
Barth	25, 119
Basel Mission	98
Bassa Country	104
Bauchi Plateau	23, 44, 45, 79, 121
Bechuanaland	10, 229, 232
Beira	23
Bell, Sir H.	107

	PAGE
Benué River	44, 51, 52, 72, 73, 75, 76, 79, 101, 102, 103, 104, 120, 163, 220, 234, 235
Berber	116, 186
Beresford	38, 42
Beriis	22, 161
Bida	168
Bingham	164, 168
Bir-Alali	131
Bison	96
Boar	91, 92
Boers	10, 208
Boney-Maury	116
Bongo	201, 202, 205
Boniface, Winifred	10
Bor	72, 86
Borku	128, 130, 131
Bornu	35, 105, 116
Botha	43, 80
Brooke, Wilmot	162, 163, 185, 189, 193
Bryce, Hon. J.	217
Buffalo	61, 63, 94
Bukuru	44, 45, 53, 168
Burmawa	48, 49
Burt	51
Burun-tunki	75

C	
CAINE, HALL	123
Cairo	160, 161, 186, 187, 231, 242
Calabar	146
Candace	165
Cape Colony	23, 97, 191, 231, 232, 233, 234
Cape Peninsula	232
Cape Province	232
Cape Town	23, 208, 232
Chad, Lake	34, 117, 120, 128, 130, 185
Chadda	191
Charga	22
Chitowe	140
Church Missionary Society	23, 39, 44, 80, 162, 168, 182, 186, 187, 189
Cleopatra	160
Columba	10

	PAGE
Conference, World's Missionary	206, 211, 212
Congo	35, 84, 97, 131, 162, 176, 177, 182, 189, 191, 194, 223, 227, 230, 233, 235
,, French	99, 230, 233
,, Belgian	35, 230
,, Valley	231
Cooper	44
Copts	115, 117, 161
Crane	75
Crocodiles	86
Crown Bird	75
Crowther, Bishop	10, 162, 185, 189

D	
DACHLA	22, 129
Dahabiah, Nile	76
Dan, Dangana	78, 94, 173, 174
Darfur	116, 119, 235
Dar-Kuti	94, 225
Delagoa Bay	23
Dempar	12, 13, 44, 50, 51, 52, 53
Derwish	116, 129, 204
Dinka	7, 86
Djebel-Abu-Koubeis	126
Djen	77, 79
Djengis-khan	14
Dodo	12, 13
Dogeri	51, 136
Dogon-kurmi	50
Doleib Hill	168
Donga	44, 53
Dongola	167, 186
Dove, Prof.	23
Duck	75, 76
Dutch Mission	186
Dutch East India Company	231
Durban	232

E	
EGBE	168
Egypt	24, 33, 37, 115, 117, 118, 124, 129, 136, 159, 160, 161, 165, 187, 231, 242
Egypt General Mission	186, 187

INDEX

	PAGE
Egyptians	4, 10
Entebbe	183
Elephant	61, 65, 86, 92, 93, 94, 97, 98
Elliott, Capt.	39
Emlyn, Dr.	45, 53
Ennedi	131
Eratosthenes	192
Erythrea	165
Ethiopia,	29, 141, 157, 165, 166, 167, 188
Ethiopian Movement	233
Evans	43, 45

	PAGE
FADAMA	64
Fayoum	22
Fez	126
Fezzan, Turkish	35
Fingal	232
Florence Bay	182
Fort Archambault	224, 226
Freetown	123
Fulah	118, 120, 228
Fulanchi	155
Fulani	65, 100, 220, 221, 222

	PAGE
GALLA COUNTRY	97, 230, 231
Garanganze	180
Garstang, Prof.	166, 167
Garua	38
Gazelle	183
Gazum	48, 49
Gebel-Grurian	22
Gezira	115
Giraffe	93, 94, 97, 183
Girkawa	48
Girouard, Sir P.	41, 43
Giwa	58
Gobat, Bishop	162, 181, 185
Gobar	120
Gold Coast	189, 229
Gongola	79
Gordon, General	237, 238, 240
Goshen	159
Guardafui	119
Guinea Coast	23

	PAGE
Guinness, Dr. H. Grattan	163, 214
Guinter	53, 156
Gwynne, Bishop	123, 205, 228, 239
Gyptic	161

	PAGE
HABISCH	98
Haj	111
Hamitic	12
Harris, Hermann	164
Harris, Kendell	164
Hartebeest	60, 93
Hausa	10, 20, 22, 40, 52, 65, 76, 77, 78, 79, 81, 104, 107, 120, 164, 185, 220, 222
Hausaland	37, 116
Herodotus	166
Hill, Bishop	164
Hippo	86, 95, 97
Hosking	43, 75, 77, 78, 79, 80, 90
Hottentot	232
Hyena	64, 104

	PAGE
IBN-KHALDUM	117
Ibrahim	98
Ibi	44, 50, 51, 52, 53, 100, 101, 220
Igalwa	144
Ituri	87

	PAGE
JARUB	128
Jebba	168
Johannesburg	232
Juju hill	48
Jukun	12, 52, 53

	PAGE
KAABA	126
Kabir	168
Kadiriya	120
Kaduna	40
Kakanda	102

Kalahari Desert	191
Khalid	116
Kamerun	85, 140, 233
Kanem	116, 118, 130, 131
Kano	119
Kanuri	185
Katsa	168
Kavirondo	231
Keffi Gengi	226
Kelu	108
Kenia Mount	140, 183, 231
Khalifa	129
Khama	10
Khartum	33, 87, 115, 123, 129, 167, 168, 186, 202, 205, 228, 239
Kibyen	45, 49
Kijabe	23
Kilimanjaro	183
Kimberley	43
Kingsley, Mary	141, 143
Koran	109, 124, 125, 127, 196
Kordofan	116, 119, 120
Koelle	180, 185
Kotto	27, 225
Kpada	168
Kura,	104, 105
Kusseri	38
Kuta	168
Krapf	181, 182, 192
Laka	99
Lagos	164, 234

LAGOS - KANO Railroad, 41

Lam Pagans	83, 85
Langtang	44, 48, 53, 168
Lenz, Dr. Oscar	118, 228, 229
Leopard	64, 92
Lewis, Wm.	11
Liberia	234
Libyan Desert	24, 115, 128, 129, 130
Lion	64, 92
Livingstone	180, 181, 191, 192, 193
Livingstonia	181
Livingstone Inland Mission	181
Lokoja	39, 43, 103, 163, 168, 220
Lovedale	188
Lualaba	35, 231
Lucy Memorial Freed Slaves' Home	38, 42, 43, 44, 45, 79, 103, 190
Luxor	186

MACCARTHY, Gen.	147
Mackay	193, 194
Mahdi	116, 120
Malay	232
Mandara	121
Mandjafa	82
Manning, Cardinal	5
Marabuts	228
Marra	121
Martin	53
Marua	83, 85
Massai	24
Matabeleland	229
Mauritania	117
Maxwell	43, 98, 155
M'bula	44, 79, 168
McNaught, Miss	107
Mecca	58, 93, 94, 95, 126, 226, 227
Meroe	165
Moffat	181, 182, 192
Mohammed Othman	120
Mohammed El Tounsey	192
Mohgul	14
Mombasa	23, 182, 183
Mongol	6, 12, 14
Montoil	48
Moon, Mountains of the	183
Moot	129
Morocco	115, 116, 126, 130, 187
Mostaganem	126
Mosquitoes	86
Mozambique	23
Muhamed-Ben-Ali	126
Mukawkas	117
Munchi	218, 219, 220, 221
Murchison Range	23, 44, 48, 121

INDEX

	PAGE
Mureji	40
Musa	172, 173
Musgan	7, 83, 218, 219, 221
Musgrave, Miss	107
Murzuk	128

NAIROBI ... 23
   Nassarawa ... 38
Nassau, Dr. 142, 143, 146, 148
Natal ... 23
Ndele ... 96
Ndorko ... 147
Ngaumdere ... 99, 132
Ngaumdere Laka ... 99
Ngell ... 44, 45
Niger ... 27, 29, 40, 117, 118, 163, 185, 191, 234
Niger Co. ... 51, 220, 221
Niger, Lower ... 35
Nigeria, Northern 12, 22, 23, 24, 29, 36, 37, 39, 74, 81, 98, 102, 103, 130, 136, 168, 185, 195, 218, 220, 221, 224, 229
Nigeria, Southern 39, 229
Nile 27, 29, 35, 52, 93, 166, 168, 183, 191, 223, 226, 234, 235, 240
Nile, Blue 115, 165, 166, 167
Nile Delta ... 33
Nile Valley ... 33, 115
Nile, White ... 85
Npambe ... 140
Nubia ... 22, 37
Numan ... 79
Nyangwe ... 35
Nyassa, Lake ... 122
Nyassaland 122, 188, 231
Nyam-Nyam 218, 219, 222, 223

OMAN ... 119
   Omdurman 158, 202
Orange River Colony 23, 231
Ormuz ... 135

Othman ... 120
Orwaldler, Brother ... 162

PACHYDERMS ... 97
   Panyam ... 44, 168
Paiko ... 168
Park, Mungo ... 191
Patagi ... 168
Pfaender, Dr. 181, 185, 186
Pelican ... 75
Penates ... 140
Peter ... 171, 172
Petrie, Prof. ... 165
Pickthall, Marmaduke ... 123
Pigmies ... 87
Pioneer Camp ... 50, 51
Pliny ... 192
Polygamy ... 157, 176, 177
Poncho ... 25
Port Elizabeth ... 232
Ptolemies ... 160
Ptolemy ... 192
Pyramid, Great ... 159

QUADROON ... 98
   Quorra ... 107

RABBA ... 132
   Ramadan ... 126, 138
Ratzel ... 148, 176
Rebman ... 181, 182
Reclus ... 149
Red Sea ... 118
Rembwé ... 147
Rhinos ... 97
Richardson ... 194
Rift Valley ... 231
Rock Station ... 44, 49, 50
Rohlfs ... 25, 128
Rosebery, Lord ... 242
Rudolf, Lake ... 231
Rumasha 38, 44, 53, 102, 168
Ruwenzori ... 183

U

SAHARA 35, 97, 115, 116, 119, 120, 128, 138, 164, 191, 227
Said, the Fisherman ... 123
Sara-Kabba 218, 219, 222
Scottish Mission... .. 231
Senaar 120
Senegal ... 131, 162, 234
Shari 34, 82, 121, 226, 227, 234, 235
Shari Chad Protectorate 35, 84, 130, 131, 218, 224
Shari Valley 85
Sharpe, Sir A. 122
Sheba, Queen of... ... 165
Shire 34
Shilluk 7
Shonga 168
Sidi Ahmed 130
Sidi Barrani ... 130, 131
Sidi-el-Mahdi ... 128, 129
Sidi-Mohammed-Sunni... 129
Sidi Muhamed 127
Sierra Leone 123, 130, 229, 234
Sinussi .. 85, 94, 121, 127, 128, 129, 130, 131, 213
Sinussiism 126
Sinussi Ndele 130
Slave ... 98, 99, 100, 101, 102, 109
Slave Raiding ... 213, 221
Snipe 75
Soha 167
Sokoto 120
Songhai 116, 118
Sphinx ... 3, 237, 242
Stanford 35
Stanley 84, 182
Stork 75
Strabo 192
Suahili 230, 231
Sudan ... 33, 35, 36, 37, 44, 52, 81, 84, 87, 97, 129, 131, 133, 151, 157, 162, 165, 167, 222, 227, 239, 240, 241
Sudan, Anglo-Egyptian 29, 33, 35, 218, 223, 225, 229
Sudan, Central 82, 85, 163, 164

Sudan, Eastern 33, 85, 130, 164, 167, 168, 205
Sudan, French Western 35, 36
Sudan Interior Mission ... 168
Sudan, North ... 121, 224
Sudan Pioneer Mission ... 186
Sudan United Mission 23, 36 38, 39, 42, 43, 44, 48, 49, 75, 80, 98, 168, 190, 220
Sudan, Western 33, 185, 228
Sudd Region 85, 86, 121, 230
Suras, Mecca 125
Suras, Medina 125
Swaziland 231

TAJURA 119
Tangele 79
Tanganyika ... 182, 231
Taylor, Hudson 214
Teal ... .- 76
Thebes 165
Thornton 187
Tibesti 130
Timbuktu... 33, 35, 116, 118, 162, 163, 191, 226
Tijani 120
Tom 44, 103
Tonnelet 26
Tours 113
Transvaal... 23, 231, 232
Tripoli 22, 24, 52, 115, 117, 127, 128, 130, 164, 187
Tuareck 118, 131
Tubus 131
Tucker, Bishop 184
Tunis ... 22, 115, 130, 187
Tacitus 151

UBANGI 162
Uganda ... 23, 24, 34, 97, 89, 182, 184, 188, 189, 190, 195, 234
Ukerewe 182
Ulfilas 10
Ursa Major ... 65, 69
Ursa Minor ... 65, 69

INDEX

	PAGE
VICTORIA, LAKE...	23, 182, 231
Vischer, Hans	84
WADAI	116, 119, 128, 131, 132
Wahabi	120
Wady-Halfa	186
Wallace, Sir W. ...	40, 103
Wasé	48, 136
Washington, Booker	10, 11, 179, 215
White, Silva ...	132, 149, 176
Winkelried, Arnulf von	241
Wukari	44, 53, 100, 136, 168
Wushishi... ...	43, 168

	PAGE
YERGUM ...	48, 49
Yola Province	80, 81, 101
Yoruba ...	10, 185, 188, 189
Young ...	... 43
Yussif	159, 160
ZAIRE	162
Zambesi	34, 35, 97, 176
Zanzibar ...	... 23, 117, 119
Zaria	168
Zebras	97, 183
Zegi	103
Zimmerman	80
Zöller, Dr. Hugo ...	228
Zulu	7, 24
Zululand	229
Zunguru ...	38, 39, 40, 41, 42, 43, 106

www.ingramcontent.com/pod-product-compliance
Lightning Source LLC
Chambersburg PA
CBHW031421150426
43191CB00006B/351